GREAT BAR FOOD
AT HOME

GREAT BAR FOOD
AT HOME

KATE HEYHOE

PHOTOGRAPHS BY ALEXANDRA GRABLEWSKI

1807
WILEY
2007

JOHN WILEY & SONS, INC.

Wiley Bicentennial Logo Design: Richard J. Pacifico

Published by John Wiley & Sons, Inc., Hoboken, New Jersey
Published simultaneously in Canada

Design by Elizabeth Van Itallie

Library of Congress Cataloging-in-Publication Data:

Heyhoe, Kate.
 Great bar food at home / Kate Heyhoe.
   p. cm.
 Includes index.
 ISBN: 978-0-471-78183-7 (cloth)

1. Appetizers. I. Title.
TX740.H487 2007
641.8'12–dc22

                             2006032485

Printed in China
10 9 8 7 6 5 4 3 2 1

To Alma Shon, who puts the "happy" in happy hour
and is proof positive that life should be shaken, not stirred.
Thanks for lifting our spirits every day, in every way.

CONTENTS

CHEERS TO THE GOOD LIFE

Frank Sinatra, Louis Armstrong, Jackie O, and other celebrities often wound up their evenings at P.J. Clarke's, ordering a nightcap and a late-night snack. In 2003, the legendary saloon on the corner of Third Avenue and 55th Street on Manhattan's East Side was restored. New owners Timothy Hutton and partners installed modern fixtures, an updated menu and more space, but P.J.'s bartenders still serve half-shells of raw clams and oysters on the original century-old oak bar (which also appeared in Billy Wilder's classic film, *The Lost Weekend*). Food and drink flow freely, and the ambiance remains warm and welcoming, if not a little rowdy at times.

Across the nation in Napa Valley, casual but upscale wine bars, with patios overlooking vineyards, set out "bocconcini per vini"—little dishes of house-cured meats, olives, and salmon, cheeses and breads, or small meals of pizza and panini with the finest regional red and white wines served by the glass—in the tradition of the Italian enoteca and the French wine bar.

During happy hour in Chicago, dozens of breweries pack patrons in with bowls of Asiago dip, toasted beer bread, hot nachos, and pints of handcrafted ales. From Montreal to Austin, local brewpubs, decked out in warm wood and copper tanks, plate up chicken wings, barbecued salmon, mustard-slathered sausages, and salty garlic fries.

Coast to coast, these establishments, like the diverse and legendary hangouts, lounges and clubs of the present and past century—'21', the Rainbow Room, the Stork Club, Enrico's, to name a few—provide the famous, the infamous, and the everyday person with a second home: a warm, friendly place to enjoy a drink, a nibble, or a nosh. Nothing too fancy or fussy. Just a comfortable atmosphere with refreshments that go down easy.

Wouldn't it be great to enjoy yourself this same way, in the comfort of your own home? Whether you're unwinding from work or celebrating the weekend with a classic cocktail, a glass of wine, or a pint of ale, a little dish of something special or a bowl of crunchy nibbles makes all the difference in the world between ho-hum feeding and civilized living.

Bartenders don't have time to be fussy with food. They either pour out salty, ready-to-eat snacks, or send orders to a prep kitchen for more elaborate goodies. At home, when you're the bartender, cook, and patron all rolled into one, only certain types of bar food make sense: ones that can be made in advance, or require just a quick heat or reheat; seasoned tidbits poured into a dish and eaten with fingers; or perhaps a small, simple plate that doubles as a snack or light meal.

Dim the lights, pull up a stool, and pour a drink. Rack up the CDs or turn on the Big Game. Then relax—and enjoy the evening with Great Bar Food at Home. Life is good.

BAR BITES: COZY COMFORTS OF THE HOME BAR

This is not a book about how to mix drinks. It's about what to eat after the drinks are mixed, poured, or uncapped . . . You won't learn here how to become a master bartender, a sommelier, or a brewmaster. But if you do drink, this book will make the cocktail, wine, or beer you sip a more rewarding and pleasurable experience. It's all about being kind to yourself with good food, good drink, and pure enjoyment, in the cozy atmosphere of your own home.

These recipes are stress-free, easy, and meant to be made and eaten casually (many of them can be prepared in advance). Their appeal lies in their robust flavors, serving simplicity, and the way the recipes complement each section's beverages—cocktail food, wine food, and beer food—but you can also eat them with any beverage of choice. They're the same type of tasty nibbles found at all the best bars—and they can look and taste just as tempting, even when made at home.

Why I Wrote This Book

At a certain age, my tribal instincts changed. I found myself preferring to pass time with a special person or a small cadre of close friends, rather than bar hopping or hosting big parties. But my style of entertaining at home (whether just with my mate or with outside guests) doesn't mean doting on trivial presentations, labor-intensive hors d'oeuvres, or meticulously crafted finger foods—nor does it mean slacking about with bags of Doritos and jars of salsa.

I wanted excitingly bold, robust flavors, the kind served at my favorite bars—but, being the bartender and cook, I also wanted them easy to prepare and serve. Still, they had to be treats in the truest sense. Pure pleasure. Small bites to look forward to, and ones which elevate the act of imbibing a cocktail, a glass of wine, or a craft beer into a gratifying sensory event. This is the collection I created, and I hope it finds a pleasurable path into your routine as well.

I also believe the home bar, with enticing food and drink, is the social wave of the century. With stricter drinking and driving penalties, in a fuel-strapped, post–9/11 world, the option of enjoying a cocktail at home rather than at a bar makes sense. Digitally sophisticated sound and home entertainment systems, iPod-driven playlists, more living space, kitchens that function as the hub of the house, and increasingly accommodating conveniences have made the home a pretty comfortable place to be. Now, all one needs is a few snappy dishes with sophistication and style, like the ones in these pages, to make the evening complete.

As a last word, I also enjoy the cocktail hour accompanied by assorted mental vacations and conversation-starters (often leading to a Google or Wikipedia excursion). So aside from the recipes, this book is peppered with tales of bygone times, romance, and social tidbits. It conjures up images of Hollywood in its heyday, risqué rendezvous in gin joints, and basking in *la bella vita*.

Even if you never cook from this book, I hope you'll still experience it. Flip through the pages for tidbits of inspiration, vicarious enjoyment, and carefree entertainment. Set it out on the bar: someone is sure to pick it up.

PAIRING FOOD WITH COCKTAILS, WINE, AND BEER

What's your "usual"? Most folks gravitate to one, or maybe two, favorite beverages on a regular basis: you might be a Scotch man, a daiquiri dame, a Pinot Noir or Chardonnay geek, a stout or lager lover. The dishes you crave, though, may stretch from Bombay to Zimbabwe, or may be different every night of the week. So drink what you want, and enjoy the foods you like. After all, it's your bar: You're the main guest, so order whatever you please!

If you do want to match bar bites to beverages, there's no need to get overly complicated: Follow the simple tips below, but keep in mind that your own personal preferences take precedent over anyone's tips or guidelines.

Savor the Flavor: Pairing Fundamentals

Fortunately the basic rules of pairing foods to beverages apply to all three alcohol categories—cocktails, wine, and beer: When it comes to flavor, match like with like, or strive for contrast (as in balancing sweet against sour, or using acidity to cut richness).

Whether you're sipping wine, cocktails, or beer, focus on the actual flavors in the glass (don't just sip—let your nose be a guide and take a whiff) and proceed to pair your food from there. This is especially important with cocktails.

With mixed cocktails, the mixer usually dominates the flavor—be it ginger ale in a Moscow Mule, orange juice in a screwdriver, or sweetened lime juice in a gimlet. With straight spirits, alcohol hits the taste buds like a locomotive, so you need power-packed or rich, oily flavors to soften the impact. (Strong buttery cheeses, for instance, do well with straight Scotch whiskey and cognac.)

Because the subtleties of complex wines can get lost with bold and bright cocktail fare, I find that a simple, straightforward wine is often best with bar food. On the other hand, the more unique the beer, especially today's innovative craft beers, the more it seems to dance with sprightly little bar bites.

Others may emphasize the nuances of pairing in greater detail, but at the risk of oversimplifying, the fundamentals boil down to common-sense logic:

1. The goal when matching food to beverage is to bring out the best in both: Strive to pair flavors that are either contrasting or complementary. Let neither food nor beverage overwhelm the other. When it comes to picking the right flavor and intensity, try thinking of the beverage as a condiment to the food. Generally speaking, you should match strong-flavored beverages with strong-flavored foods, and milder beverages with more delicate foods.

2. The same goes for textures: Put together contrasting or complementary textures in both food and drink. Dark ales, piña coladas, and cheese dips tend to the heavy or denser side of the scale, while chilled sake and Salmon Tartar are lighter in texture. Texture in wine can be considered as body, so select on a scale from light to heavy.

3. When it comes to food texture, bar bites that go "crunch!" seem to fit all beverage categories. And who can resist crunch? The liquid equivalent of crunchy foods is effervescence—sparkling wines, club soda, beer, carbonated mixers. They tickle the palate and lift the flavors of both the drink and the food.

4. Focus on palate refreshment. If the flavors of either the drink or the food are too heavy, cleanse the palate with something acidic, like lime in a bar bite or beverage. Beers and sparkling wines with their palate-cleansing bubbles also work well.

5. If your goal is to stimulate the appetite, stick with lighter nibbles (like baked Seeded Honey Crisps on page 42 rather than Garlic Fries on pages 106 and 108) and lighter drinks (like apéritifs rather than stout).

Remember: The overall flavor of the drink, not the specific liquor, matters most in food pairing. Match the mixer to the food, unless, of course, you're drinking your spirits straight. Likewise, the dominant flavor of the bar bite is more important than the main ingredient: coconut shrimp is sweet, but shrimp ceviche is tart and salty, yet both feature shrimp as the main ingredient.

Just as some food recipes use wines and spirits as flavorings, some of today's exotic mixed cocktails feature common cooking ingredients. So matching beverages to dishes that contain those same ingredients is easy (in a like-with-like sense). Try a Green Apple-tini with Green Apple–Cucumber Matchsticks (page 38), for instance. Or drink a Kir with Salmon Cassis (page 87), since both contain the same black currant liqueur.

Bar Food and Beverage Pairing Guide

Bar bites tend to be assertively seasoned, mainly because their beverage buddies demand big, bold flavors. And bar bites were designed to keep people drinking, so salty and spicy are a working bartender's best friends.

When it comes to dining, most folks start with food and select the wine or other beverage to match. But not at the bar. When the barkeep asks, "What will you have?" the patron generally orders a specific cocktail, wine, or beer. Then come the bar bites, often ordered while already sipping a drink.

So, in the belief that most folks pick their bar beverage first (typically their "usual"), I've organized this guide according to the dominant flavor of the drink. Find where your drink fits, and then pick the food flavors to match. If your beverage of choice is a . . .

➤ **BITTER DRINK**—Wines high in tannins are also more bitter, and pair well with bar bites that have their own degree of bitterness, as in grilled or charred foods, and with oily or fatty ingredients, like cheese. Paprika, arugula, chicory, caraway, and cumin all have an edge of bitterness to them. Bitterness or astringency in cocktails and beer follows the same rule. Bar bites with a pronounced sweetness, like Char Shu Slices with Mahogany Marmalade and Hot Mustard (page 111), in turn, lend balance to bitter drinks, and offset astringency. Hops are the main bitter component in beer, and bitter beers taste great balanced with a bite on the sweet side.

➤ **OAK AND SMOKE**—Oaky wines, smoky spirits, and roasted malt beers need strong mates to stand up to their pronounced flavors. Caramelized foods, vanilla essences, barbecue, and smoked foods make good comrades.

➤ **SALTY DRINK**—Alcohol plays tricks on the tongue, amplifying the perception of spices and salt. Red wines don't actually contain salt, but ones with high tannin levels exaggerate salty flavors. So a drink with a hefty alcohol punch (or a tannic red wine like Cabernet or Zinfandel) makes food taste saltier. These drinks, and salt-rimmed cocktails, favor bold flavors that can hold their own against the power of salt, whether they be spicy, sweet, acidic, or a combination. To match like-with-like, tomatoes are high in sodium, so a Bloody Mary and tomato-based bar bites (like Teacup Tomato Toasts, page 65) are both on the naturally salty side and taste terrific together.

➤ **SOUR DRINK**—Also known as acidity, the sourness or tartness in drinks contrasts well with oily and rich foods, like deep-fried foods and rich sauces. In matching like-with-like, acidity in drink also marries well to acidity in food, as with citrus and vinegar flavors. Interestingly, acidic drinks (such as gimlets) can magnify the flavors of subtle foods, and they're good complements to salty snacks. As wines go, Sauvignon Blanc, Chardonnay, or dry Riesling pairs well with tart foods. American pale ales have citrus-y tones, perfect for lime flavors in Mexican food, while the acidity in hops balances richness, as in aged cheeses.

➤ **SWEET DRINK**—Mid-range sweetness calls for spicy-hot bar bites, or salty ones. Soy sauce is a natural contrast to sweetness, so Asian dishes can handle a drink on the mildly sweet side, such as an off-dry Gewürztraminer or Riesling. Malty, sweet dark lagers like to party with caramelized onions, as both share a similar sweetness level. On the other hand, if the drink is in the dessert-sweet range, serve it with a food that's as sweet or slightly less so. Blue-veined cheeses and dates merit from a fruity wine on the sweetish side, like port, or a barley wine style of ale. Rich, buttery Gorgonzola also balances fruity-sweet cocktails, especially those with berry tones, like blackberry or currant flavored daiquiris. Sweet cocktails like Cosmopolitans kiss up to Parmigiano-Reggiano. Stout, with its roasted coffee and chocolate tones, and fruit beers (including Belgian lambics) bring out the best in bar bites on the sweet side, or even dessert bites.

A Note on Cheeses: Dairy products in general soften the impact of alcohol and temper its harshness. Cheeses with rich, buttery tones make ideal contrasts to the wide range of beer, wine, and cocktails. Cheeses can help balance sweetness, and they can also add a salty or acidic note, as in feta and goat cheeses. So even if the cheeses aren't being eaten straight off the cheese board, if they're a driving flavor in the dish, use them as markers for selecting the beverage.

Don't know where your drink fits—especially when buying an unfamiliar wine or beer? Here's a tip: Watch the descriptors. How is the wine, beer, or cocktail described? When words like melon, spice, pepper, chocolate, and smoke describe the beverage, then pick food flavors that echo or contrast these descriptors.

COCKTAIL
BITES AND
CLASSIC
CLUB FARE...

Smart cocktails deserve stylish little dishes, the kind found in timeless bars, historic hangouts, and clubs with atmosphere . . .

Sip to the rattle of martinis being shaken, not stirred, by bartenders in crisp white shirts and black vests. These rooms charm us with their cozy, comfy, and often classy atmosphere, serving food in dimly lit (but not *too* dimly lit) rooms. Catering to Café Society in one era, and watering holes for writers, artists, beatniks, and billionaires in another. Such intimate spots (many now long gone) were like cocktail spas: places to relax and unwind, with plush leather chairs, velvet booths, and mahogany bars. Others were glamorous gossip pools, hosts in Hollywood to Liz Taylor, Ronald Reagan the actor, Nat King Cole, Lauren Bacall, or George Clooney, and in New York to Dorothy Parker, Woody Allen, Liza Minnelli, Andy Warhol, or Robert DeNiro.

Stay home, and avoid the paparazzi. These nibbles are just right for cocktails at the home bar.

Personal Caviar Tortes with Toast Points

MAKES 4 PERSONAL-SIZE TORTES

Caviar epitomizes refinement and elegance, but you don't have to break the bank to enjoy it. Splurge on expensive caviar if you like, but the two-ounce jars of lumpfish caviar stocked in supermarkets work just fine in this affordable indulgence.

Each individual disk of seasoned cream cheese, topped with caviar, is the right size for one or two people. Make the cream cheese foundations up to three days in advance, then top them off with caviar right before serving.

8 ounces cream cheese, at room temperature
2 tablespoons fresh dill, plus extra for garnish
2 cloves garlic, minced
4 teaspoons fresh lemon juice
½ teaspoon salt
⅛ teaspoon white pepper
One 2-ounce jar black caviar, chilled

SERVE WITH
Toast Points (see Note), cocktail bread, or
crackers

1. In a bowl, mix the cream cheese, dill, garlic, lemon juice, salt, and white pepper together. Line four 1-cup ramekins with plastic wrap. Pack the cheese mixture evenly into each ramekin, to make 4 short disks. Pull the sides of the plastic up, and seal the mixtures. Refrigerate for 4 hours or up to 3 days.

2. Unwrap the disks and set them on individual serving plates. With your fingers, press each top down to create a depression, leaving a rim around the edge to help hold in the caviar (kind of like shaping a moon crater). Spoon the caviar on top of each torte, garnish with dill, and serve.

TOAST POINTS: Preheat the oven to 300°F. To make 12 points, remove the crust from 6 slices thin white sandwich bread, and slice the bread on the diagonal, into triangles. Arrange the triangles on a baking sheet. Bake 5 to 7 minutes, turning once, until dry and toasted. Cool on a wire rack. (May be refrigerated in an airtight container for up to 1 week.)

Gougère

MAKES FIFTEEN 1 1/2-INCH PUFFS

When *New York* magazine sought out the city's Best Amuse-Bouche in 2004, here's what made them swoon:

"Gougères, those wonderfully light cheese puffs, have been elevated to new heights by chef de cuisine Didier Elena at Alain Ducasse, where the little Burgundian delicacies get a surprise creamy cheese filling. The airy, puffy choux pastry shell, flavored with comte cheese from the Jura, is filled with Mornay sauce while still hot and crisp, then served immediately on a silver-edged Lalique plate as a welcoming hors d'oeuvre with an apéritif. Avoid the temptation to take a bite. The cheese might ooze and ruin the evening. Happily, they're small enough to pop into the mouth whole for an unexpectedly intense cheesy sensation."

For easy, casual cocktail bites at home, you can skip the Lalique plate and the extra step of a Mornay sauce. Even without the fancy trimmings, these plain little gougères just may take up permanent residence on your bar bite menu. The pastries can be cooked, frozen, and reheated, and, as the review above suggests, they lend themselves well to all sorts of creative variations (try white Cheddar and diced jalapeños for a Southwest twist).

½ cup water
½ stick (4 tablespoons) salted butter
⅛ teaspoon white pepper
½ cup all-purpose flour
2 large eggs
½ teaspoon Dijon mustard
2 ounces Gruyère cheese, finely grated

1. Preheat the oven to 375°F. Line a baking sheet with parchment paper or grease it.

2. Heat the water, butter, and white pepper in a medium saucepan over medium-high heat. When the butter is melted and the mixture simmers, dump in the flour all at once and stir. Reduce the heat to medium and stir until the mixture pulls away from the sides of the pan, 1 to 2 minutes. Remove the pan from the heat and let the mixture cool slightly (a few seconds).

3. Add the eggs one at a time, beating well to incorporate the first egg before adding the next. Beat in the mustard and all but 2 to 3 tablespoons of the cheese. Drop by teaspoons, or pipe through a pastry bag with a half-inch tip, into 1-inch mounds an inch or more apart on the baking sheet. Sprinkle with the remaining cheese. (Tap the mounds with floured fingers to neaten or reshape them.)

4. Bake for about 25 minutes, until puffed and golden brown. Serve warm. Gougère may be sealed airtight and refrigerated for 2 days, or frozen up to 2 weeks. Reheat at 350°F for 10 minutes, or 15 minutes if frozen.

CAFÉ SOCIETY

In the late 1800s, a fashionable class of "bright young things" emerged in the cosmopolitan capitals of Paris, London, and Rome. By the 1920s, this Café Society had emerged as the "it" group of its day.

Café Society swelled out of a tradition where people of a certain class attended each other's parties, married each other's children, and traveled together to exotic resorts. They soon extended their social life to partying in public, at bars, restaurants, and clubs, making news just by being seen—especially when seen together, in charming, debonair, and well-heeled packs.

Predicated on style, not substance, Café Society chose as their heroes the entertaining chroniclers of their lives: Cole Porter, whose songs were as carefree as his audience, the Gershwins, and F. Scott Fitzgerald, who tapped into Café Society psyche with his novel *The Great Gatsby*. Women wore evening gowns and gems, men sported elegant suits and short, slick hair. Café Society's clique could be sophisticated and refined, and they could also be naughty and wild, trading in evening gowns for the leg-revealing skirts of the flappers.

Gossip columnist Cholly Knickerbocker (pen name of Maury Paul) gave these packs a name, coining the term Café Society in 1918. When Prohibition arrived, Café Society turned promptly on their fashionable heels and abandoned the fine restaurants for speakeasies, where

they could continue the carefree, party lifestyle to which they had become accustomed. Speakeasies also bore an added enticement of risqué glamour, until the day when drinking became legal again. But Café Society didn't end with Repeal. It simply staggered into the daylight and carried on as the "jet-set" and "beautiful people."

Ghee-Toasted Almonds

MAKES 1 HEAPING CUP

What's a cocktail bar without nuts? Spanish bars set out prized (and pricey) Marcona almonds toasted in olive oil, as luscious golden nibbles. The concept is supreme in its simplicity, and though Marconas are sweeter and more delicate, even common almonds shine when toasted in oil and dusted with coarse sea salt and a touch of red pepper. And when toasted in ghee instead of oil, almonds taste anything but plain.

Considered India's version of clarified butter, ghee can be found in specialty stores and some supermarkets. But unlike traditional clarified butter, which comes from whole milk, ghee starts with butter churned from slightly soured milk, leaving it mildly tart. When clarifying the butter, Indian cooks also toast the milk solids slightly before straining them away, infusing the ghee with a delightfully nutty undertone that comes out best when warmed. But if you don't have ghee, stick with a fruity olive oil for flavor.

For spice, add a few pinches of your favorite ground red chile. I prefer the seductive Aleppo pepper, but cayenne, paprika (smoked or regular), chipotle, and New Mexican chiles work well, too.

1 tablespoon ghee (or olive oil)
6 ounces (1 heaping cup) blanched almonds
Sea salt to taste
Aleppo pepper, or other ground red chile pepper to taste

1. Heat the ghee (or olive oil) in a skillet just large enough to hold the almonds in a single layer, over medium heat.

2. Add the almonds to the pan and cook, stirring often, until the almonds turn a rich, toasty golden color (as long as 10 minutes). Sprinkle with salt and a few pinches of red pepper. Pour the almonds onto a plate to cool slightly. They taste best warm, so reheat if necessary (in a skillet, or in a microwave oven 1 to 2 minutes on High). Store in an airtight container for up to 1 week.

My Blue Heaven Spread

MAKES ABOUT 1 1/4 CUPS

I have to admit when I was creating this recipe, I got a little tipsy (ah, the joyful hazards of recipe testing!). I made three variations—one with Port, one with Marsala, and one with crème de cassis—tasting each one frequently to come up with the best recipe. All of these flavorings work fine with Gorgonzola, but in the end, the crème de cassis (made from black currants) produced the most complex taste: slightly sweet with deep berry tones. Still, don't tie yourself to these ingredients; you can make a fine, rich-tasting spread using whichever of these spirits you have on hand, and don't be afraid to substitute Roquefort, Stilton, or any other blue-veined cheese. For best results, I don't recommend any substitution for the hazelnuts, as their unique flavor sets this recipe apart from other spreads. Serve it with crostini, crackers, or apple slices.

4 ounces Gorgonzola or other blue-veined cheese, at room temperature
3 ounces (¾ stick) unsalted butter, softened (preferably European-style butter)
1 tablespoon crème de cassis
⅛ teaspoon allspice, plus extra for garnish
Dash white pepper
¼ cup coarsely chopped, toasted hazelnuts (see Note)

1. Using a fork, mash together the cheese, butter, cassis, allspice, and white pepper until the mixture is completely blended. Stir in the hazelnuts, reserving a small amount for garnish.

2. Cover and refrigerate, then bring to room temperature and garnish with another dash of allspice and the reserved nuts before serving. The spread will keep 5 days, refrigerated.

TOASTED HAZELNUTS: If you don't find toasted hazelnuts in your store, make your own—it's worth toasting a large batch of nuts, then freezing them for use in other recipes. To toast and skin hazelnuts, preheat the oven to 350°F. Spread shelled hazelnuts on a baking sheet in a single layer. Bake 10 to 15 minutes, until the skins crackle. Then wrap up the hazelnuts in an old, clean towel and let them steam for 5 to 10 minutes. Rub them vigorously in the towel until the skins flake off. (Tip: Rub the skins outdoors for easy cleanup, as the flakes can get messy.) Don't be concerned if some of the skin stays on—it adds a pleasant contrasting color and flavor.

'21' Club's Crab Cakes with Cucumber-Ginger Salad

BY EXECUTIVE CHEF STEPHEN TROJAHN

SERVES 4 (1 CRAB CAKE PER PERSON) AS SUBSTANTIAL BAR BITES

Crab cakes never go out of style. At the '21' Club, Executive Chef Stephen Trojahn serves what may be the most classic of all bar bites, from what many consider to be New York's classiest bar.

At '21', the chef boils the crabs from scratch, and shapes the patties with ring molds. Home cooks can use eight ounces of lump crab from the seafood counter or a pasteurized container, and shape the cakes in ramekins, or similar molds. When you mix the crabmeat mixture together, don't be alarmed if it looks way too soupy. I found that when the formed cakes were chilled for thirty to forty-five minutes, they held their shape well and the results were outstanding. You'll need an ovenproof skillet for this recipe.

VEGETABLE MIXTURE
2 tablespoons olive oil
1 tablespoon minced fresh jalapeño
½ cup minced red bell pepper
½ cup minced onion
⅛ teaspoon sea salt, or to taste
⅛ teaspoon freshly ground white pepper, or to taste

CRAB CAKES
2 large egg yolks
2 tablespoons lime juice
1 tablespoon Tabasco sauce
5 tablespoons mayonnaise
2 tablespoons Dijon mustard
1 tablespoon chopped chives
2 teaspoons finely chopped cilantro
1½ teaspoons finely chopped flat leaf parsley
Pinch cayenne pepper
8 ounces cooked crabmeat, in knuckle-sized chunks
½ cup soft breadcrumbs
¼ cup Panko breadcrumbs, plus 1 cup for breading
¼ cup olive oil
3 sprigs lemon thyme
1 tablespoon unsalted butter

SERVE WITH
Cucumber Ginger Salad (optional; see recipe on page 28)

1. Prepare the vegetable mixture: Warm 2 tablespoons olive oil in an oven-proof skillet over medium-low heat. Add the jalapeño, bell pepper, onion, salt, and white pepper. Cook the vegetables (do not brown them), stirring occasionally, until translucent, about 5 minutes. Remove from the heat and let the vegetables cool.

2. Prepare the crab cakes: In a mixing bowl, combine the yolks, lime juice, and Tabasco and mix well. Add the mayonnaise, mustard, chives, cilantro, parsley, and cayenne and whisk well. Stir in the crabmeat and the vegetable mixture. Add the soft breadcrumbs, and $\frac{1}{4}$ cup Panko crumbs. Mix well.

3. Set out four $3\frac{1}{2}$-inch ramekins. For each ramekin, line with plastic wrap, layer 2 tablespoons Panko crumbs in the bottom, followed by $\frac{1}{4}$ of the crab mixture, and another 2 tablespoons Panko. Pat the mixture down and seal tightly with the plastic wrap. Refrigerate about 45 minutes until chilled, so the cakes keep their shape. Shake any loose Panko off before dropping the cakes into the skillet.

4. Preheat the oven to 375°F. Warm $\frac{1}{4}$ cup olive oil in an ovenproof skillet over medium heat, until semi-hot (a few crumbs gently sizzle). Carefully add the crab cakes to the pan, cook slowly for about $3\frac{1}{2}$ minutes, then turn them over. (Be gentle when you flip them. Their chunkiness makes them a tad fragile.) Add the thyme springs and butter to the pan, place in the oven, and cook for approximately $3\frac{1}{2}$ minutes, or until golden brown. Remove from the pan. Serve immediately, with Cucumber Ginger Salad.

Cucumber Ginger Salad

1 cup peeled, seeded, and thinly sliced cucumber
$\frac{1}{3}$ cup coarsely chopped pickled ginger
3 tablespoons pickle juice (juice that the ginger was in)
3 tablespoons rice wine vinegar
2 tablespoons chopped fresh dill, without stems
Freshly ground white pepper to taste

Mix the cucumber slices with the ginger, pickle juice, and rice vinegar. Mix in the dill, season with white pepper, and serve.

21: THE SOPHISTICATED SPEAKEASY

New York's most famous speakeasy, '21', was sometimes referred to as "the front porch"—a reference to another classic venue, the Raffles Hotel in Singapore, where it was said that if you sat on the front porch long enough, you'd meet everybody who is anybody. During its heyday, '21' wasn't just a club, it was a jolly haven for the famous, with pretzels on the bar and plenty of booze in its drinks. As author Marilyn Kaytor described '21' in her book of the same name, "The club is not a place for someone with a passion for anonymity, but, on the other hand, the house is so discreet that a lady of note can dine with her lover upstairs while her husband drinks blissfully ignorant at the bar below." Now owned by Orient-Express Hotels, the most requested private dining room at '21' is set in the famous hidden wine cellar, built during Prohibition. The cellar's ingenious two-ton door operated only when a meat skewer was placed in a tiny hole in a particular brick. The device worked so well, the Feds never found it.

Cocktail Onion'd Deviled Eggs

MAKES 12 PIECES

Cocktail onions (the pickled kind used in martinis) bring a pleasant pucker, and horseradish a perky zip, to the classic deviled egg. A resealable plastic bag has many benefits in this recipe: You can mix the yolk stuffing in it (no mess, no bowl), refrigerate the stuffing separately from the whites (leaving more space in the fridge), and use it to pipe the filling into the whites for a fancy presentation. You can also prepare the filling in the bag a day in advance, and have it ready to squeeze whenever you're ready to serve.

6 large eggs, hard-cooked (see Note)
6 cocktail onions, finely chopped
2 tablespoons prepared horseradish
4 teaspoons extra-virgin olive oil
1 tablespoon fresh lemon juice
¼ teaspoon ground white pepper
Quartered cocktail onions, paprika, celery seeds, parsley leaves, or chopped chives (optional garnish)

1. Shell the eggs, cut them in half, and pop the yolks into a resealable plastic bag (or mixing bowl). To the yolks, add the onions, horseradish, olive oil, lemon juice, and white pepper. Squeeze the air from the bag and seal. Mash the yolk mixture until combined. Chill until ready to use.

2. Push the mixture to one corner of the bag and snip about ½ inch off that corner. Squeezing gently, fill each egg-white half. Garnish as desired and serve at room temperature, or just slightly chilled.

HARD-COOKED EGGS: Set the eggs in a single layer in a large pot. Add cold water to cover by 1 inch. Bring the water just to a boil over medium-high heat. Turn off the heat. Leave the eggs in the water for 12 minutes. Immediately plunge the eggs into a large bowl of ice water. Drain the eggs when cool, and peel.

Lighter-than-Air Nori Squares

MAKES 40 SQUARES

When I was a kid, my mother served stacks of delicate toasted nori squares as cocktail finger food. They're delightfully crisp, yet instantly melt in your mouth. Nori is seaweed, and it may sound like an odd snack, but it's got the requisite qualities for being a great cocktail nibble: It's crunchy, salty, savory, and delectably light. In fact, if you serve these paper-thin nori squares outdoors on a windy day, you'll need a paperweight to keep them from blowing away.

Anyone who's enjoyed a piece of sushi wrapped in a black strip, or a sushi hand-roll encased in a black wrapper, has eaten nori. It's also the black belt wrapped around rice crackers, more good nibbles to serve next to stacks of toasted nori. Look for packages of nori (or yakinori) with other Japanese products. Pick the large sheets, about seven inches square, for this recipe.

In a festive mood? Nori sheets cut easily with scissors, so if you're the creative type, start snipping. At Halloween, I trim the sheets into bat silhouettes, toast them up, then scatter them helter-skelter across the table as edible table decorations, paired with devilish cocktails or hot sake.

10 large sheets nori
2 to 3 teaspoons sesame or vegetable oil
About ¼ teaspoon sea salt

1. If the nori sheets are folded in half, open them up and stack them flat. Barely rub (with 2 fingers) or brush one side of each nori sheet with a thin film of oil, stacking them on top of each other as you go. Warm a dry skillet or griddle over medium heat. Drop the oiled side of the nori into the skillet. When it starts to shrivel, flip it over and cook a few more seconds. Flip back and forth as needed to complete cooking—the nori is done when it crisps and large areas turn a paler green. The first few sheets may take as long as a minute, but as the pan heats up, they'll be done in 20 seconds or less. Do not brown them or they'll taste bitter. (For best results, taste the first sheet to gauge for timing.)

2. As you cook each nori sheet, remove it to a cutting board and sprinkle with salt. Repeat the process, stacking the toasted nori sheets on top of each other and salting them as you go. With a sharp knife, cut the stack of nori sheets into 4 quarters. Set the nori squares in a shallow bowl or basket and serve. (Toasted nori will last at least a week if stored airtight at room temperature.)

DOROTHY PARKER:
QUEEN OF THE VICIOUS CIRCLE

No one proved Prohibition's failure quite as effusively as the Vicious Circle, also known as the Algonquin Round Table. The spark of their wit was typically fueled by the fire in the glass—or, during Prohibition, fire in the flask. They lunched at New York's Algonquin Hotel, and consisted of the sharpest literary tongues of the '20s, including Robert Benchley, Robert Sherwood, George S. Kaufman, Heywood Broun, Alexander Woollcott, and other regulars, but Dorothy Parker's repartee generated the most buzz coast to coast.

Dorothy Parker cut a swath of lacerating wit like no one else. "If all the girls who attended the Yale prom were laid end to end, I wouldn't be a bit surprised," she famously remarked. Her life's work stretched from theater reviews in *Vanity Fair* to book reviews in *Esquire*, penning her own books, poems, and Hollywood screenplays (prior to being blacklisted) in between.

Parker lunched at "the Gonk," but spent her nights in fashionable speakeasies like Tony Soma's (her favorite), Texas Guinan's, and Jack and Charlie's, better known as '21'. She chain-smoked Chesterfields and drank Johnny Walker Scotch, neat, but she also favored a dry Martini. After writer-actor Robert Benchley (grandfather of *Jaws* author Peter Benchley), introduced her to Orange Blossoms, Parker kept pitchers of the gin-and-orange juice-cocktail freely flowing, especially during work hours. "*Vanity Fair* colleagues became accustomed to the waves of hysterical laughter which regularly floated from Dottie's office," writes Rick English in *Modern Drunkard* magazine. (Benchley, Parker's managing editor at the time, later improvised the line "Why don't you get out of that wet coat and into a dry martini?" in Billy Wilder's film, *The Major and the Minor*.)

SELECTED DOROTHY PARKER WIT AND WISDOM:
"She looks like something that would eat its young" (referring to Dame Edith Evans).
"A little bad taste is like a nice dash of paprika."
"This is not a novel to be tossed aside lightly. It should be thrown with great force."
"She runs the gamut of emotions from A to B" (in a Broadway review of Katharine Hepburn).
"This wasn't just plain terrible, this was fancy terrible. This was terrible with raisins in it."
"The first thing I do in the morning is brush my teeth and sharpen my tongue."
"Did I enjoy the party? One more drink and I would have been under the host."

Power Rumaki with Walnut Soba Noodles

MAKES 12 RUMAKI WITH NOODLES

These meaty versions of rumaki, popularized by "Trader Vic" Bergeron, take an uptown approach to the dainty favorites of homemakers in the 1950s and '60s. Trader Vic and Don the Beachcomber both served rumaki as part of their exotic pupu platters, along with such purported Polynesian specialties as eggrolls, Crab Rangoon, and Char Shu. Despite its kitschy background, the original rendition of rumaki remains a classic bar bite, though it's sweeter than this version. These rumaki get their power punch from the thick, peppered bacon (thick-sliced bacon coated in black pepper found in specialty markets), and instead of sugary sweetness, a citrus accent cuts their richness. Soba, or Japanese buckwheat noodles, with walnut oil and balsamic vinegar, add a sophisticated, modern twist.

WALNUT SOBA NOODLES
About 4 ounces soba noodles
1 tablespoon walnut oil
1 tablespoon balsamic vinegar
2 teaspoons bottled ponzu sauce (see Note)
2 teaspoons chopped chives or scallions

RUMAKI
6 slices thick-sliced peppered bacon
**¼ cup minced scallions (both green and
   white parts)**
**6 whole chicken livers (about 12 ounces),
   halved at the natural separation**
12 canned water chestnuts
⅓ cup ponzu sauce (see Note)
Toothpicks for skewering

1. For the noodles: Bring a large pot of salted water to a boil. Add the soba noodles and cook, stirring occasionally, until the noodles are al dente (about 4 minutes; do not overcook). Drain and rinse under cold water until cool. Let drain completely. Toss the noodles with the oil, vinegar, ponzu, and chives or scallions. (Noodles may be prepared up to 2 days in advance; serve at room temperature.)

2. Halve the bacon strips by cutting them into 2 short lengths (not long, skinny strips). Set up the ingredients assembly-line style. Lay out the bacon pieces on a work surface. For each rumaki: sprinkle some scallion in the center of the bacon. Place 1 chicken liver half in the center of each bacon piece. Top with 1 water chestnut. Wrap the bacon around the filling, overlapping the ends, and secure the whole thing with a toothpick, piercing through the water chestnut to the other side of the packet.

3. Place the rumaki in a pie plate or other shallow container. Pour the ponzu sauce over them and roll them around to coat. Marinate refrigerated for 30 minutes to 4 hours, swishing them around in the sauce occasionally.

4. When ready to cook, preheat the oven to 400°F and set an oven rack in the top third of the oven. Arrange the rumaki on a rack on a pan (such as a broiler pan). Bake for 30 minutes, turning halfway through. If the bacon needs crisping, turn the heat to broil and broil just long enough to crisp it. Serve the warm rumaki on a bed of Walnut Soba Noodles, or twirl the noodles around forks and arrange them on a platter in between the rumaki.

NOTE: *Ponzu* sauce, a Japanese condiment, is also labeled as "citrus-seasoned soy sauce." Bottled versions are convenient (if only mildly authentic since they lack the treasured *yuzu* juice), and are made by Kikkoman, Mitsukan, and Eden, among other brands

HOLLYWOOD HEYDAY: TIKI TO TACKY TO WHIMSICALLY WACKY

Long before Walt Disney plunked down his first amusement park in California's rural orange groves, restaurateurs were building their own breed of fantasy lands. These glitzy palaces beckoned to Hollywood royalty, and the kitschy backgrounds made eye-catching photo-ops for stars like Lucille Ball, Sammy Davis, Jr., Katharine Hepburn, and Clark Gable.

• **THE COCOANUT GROVE (1921–1989)** recycled a Rudolph Valentino movie set for its decor. Fake palm trees from *The Sheik* "grew" in every corner and between tables, hoisting an abundance of papier-mâché coconuts and monkeys with eyes that lit up. From the blue-painted ceiling, stars twinkled over the 1,000-seat dining room. Despite the tropical theme, the menu spoke mostly French (Tournedos of Beef with Foie Gras, for instance), with a California accent of oranges, avocados, grapefruit, abalone, asparagus, and other local fare. The Cocoanut Grove is famous for being the site of the first Oscars ceremony, while the Ambassador Hotel, home of the Grove, became infamous as the place where Robert F. Kennedy, Jr. was assassinated.

• **THE BROWN DERBY (1926–1985)** opened directly across from the Ambassador Hotel, making it easy for stars to literally walk, or be chauffeured, out of the tropics, down the long driveway to Wilshire Boulevard, and back to the down-home fare of the States. The Derby food was excellent but far from exotic: Corned Beef Hash and Grapefruit Cake were key menu items, and the original Cobb Salad, a chopped salad of a dozen ingredients, was created here. The domed building was literally built in the shape of a derby, waitresses wore hoop skirts starched to look like derbies, light emanated from miniature derby fixtures, and the sign outdoors beckoned diners to "Eat in the Hat." Only one of the four Brown Derby restaurants was hat-shaped, but all were popular with the Hollywood crowd, who could often be seen lunching at the Hollywood and Vine location in costume, before returning to the nearby soundstages for yet another take.

• **DON THE BEACHCOMBER (1937–1987)** captured the romance of the South Seas, as envisioned by a Minnesota schoolteacher and her bartender husband, a former bootlegger whose island travels fueled their inspiration. Seashells, bamboo, flaming torches, and artificial rainstorms pinging off a corrugated metal roof weren't quite enough to set the ambiance. Tiki and spear-adorned theme rooms bore such names as The Black Hole of Calcutta and The Cannibal Room, and Don christened his near-lethal rum drinks with such names as the Zombie, Missionary's Downfall, and Vicious Virgin. Both Don and his arch-rival, "Trader Vic" Bergeron, claim to have created the Mai Tai, and both served flaming pupu platters of purported Polynesian appetizers, which were really gussied-up Cantonese fare. One of Don's most popular items, which gave many Americans their first taste of the canned water chestnut, was rumaki: a skewered "sarong" of bacon wrapped around a water chestnut and a chicken liver bathed in bottled Kitchen Bouquet. (Trader Vic, though, is more often credited with inventing rumaki, using a slightly different recipe.)

Green Apple–Cucumber Matchsticks

MAKES 4 SMALL SERVINGS

By itself, this matchstick salad may not seem like bar food, but it's exactly the sort of dish that brings contrast in flavor and color to the whole plate, and rounds out other bar bites. It also acts as a palate cleanser with rich or spicy foods. Try pairing small mounds of this salad with the Tangerine Yakitori (page 49), Power Rumaki (page 34), or Salmon Cassis (page 87), or with a raw bar of clams. It looks quite regal resting on a radicchio or shiso leaf.

If you have a gizmo for shredding vegetables into fine, delicate matchsticks, such as a Japanese benriner, mandoline, or special hand grater, you can make this salad in minutes. If not, use a good sharp knife.

2 tablespoons rice vinegar
1 smallish Granny Smith or other tart green apple
½ medium cucumber
2 to 3 teaspoons minced shallot
1 teaspoon walnut oil
White pepper to taste

1. Measure the rice vinegar into a medium bowl. Peel the apple, then cut the flesh into matchsticks. Toss the apple with the vinegar right away to prevent browning.

2. Peel the cucumber, remove the seeds, and cut it into matchsticks. Toss the cucumber with the apple, along with the shallot, walnut oil, and a generous pinch of white pepper.

3. Mix and taste. It should be slightly strong and astringent, but will mellow as the cucumber releases its juices. Refrigerate for 15 minutes to 3 hours. Mix again before serving.

Salmon Sliders with Lime-Sesame Mayonnaise

MAKES 8 SMALL BURGERS

Serve these plump little salmon burgers on mini-hamburger buns or small rolls. Quick cooking in a hot pan ensures a crisp, crunchy crust and a moist, rare interior. The recipe makes eight small burgers, more than the usual bar bite recipe, but any extras are great hot or cold, with or without the buns. For the mayonnaise, black sesame seeds add color, but toasted white sesame seeds may be used instead.

You'll need at least one whole lime for both the mayonnaise and the burgers—be sure to grate the lime's zest for the mayonnaise before halving the lime. And go ahead and squeeze all the juice—you'll need it for both the mayonnaise and the burgers. In this recipe, there's no need to clean the food processor's work bowl between steps. Simply scrape out the ingredients before going on to the next step.

LIME-SESAME MAYONNAISE
Grated zest of 1 lime
1 tablespoon fresh lime juice
2 teaspoons grated fresh ginger
1 teaspoon black sesame seeds
1 teaspoon toasted sesame oil
½ cup mayonnaise

SALMON SLIDERS
1 large egg
2 teaspoons fresh lime juice
2 tablespoons Dijon mustard
¾ teaspoon salt
½ teaspoon freshly ground pepper
⅓ cup toasted white sesame seeds
2 cloves garlic
2 scallions, cut in 1-inch pieces (green and white parts)
1½ pounds fresh salmon fillet
1 tablespoon canola or other neutral vegetable oil

SERVE WITH
Arugula, baby greens, or shredded lettuce
8 mini-burger buns or small rolls, buttered and toasted

1. Prepare the Lime-Sesame Mayonnaise: Combine all ingredients, mixing well. Refrigerate until ready to use.

2. Prepare the Salmon Sliders: In a large bowl, beat the egg until mixed. Measure the lime juice, mustard, salt, and pepper into the bowl.

3. Using a food processor, grind the sesame seeds to a coarse powder, resembling ground breadcrumbs or cracker crumbs. Add the ground sesame meal to the egg mixture and stir until combined.

4. Drop the garlic into the feed tube of a food processor with the blades running. When the garlic is finely chopped, drop in the scallion and process just until finely chopped (do not puree). Stir into the egg and sesame mixture.

5. Slice off and discard the salmon skin, and pull out any pin bones. Chunk the salmon into roughly 1-inch cubes and place in the food processor. Pulse in bursts until the salmon is coarsely chopped into small pieces about the size of corn kernels. (Don't turn the salmon into a paste; small chunks add texture.) Scrape the salmon into the bowl with the egg and sesame mixture. Stir until well mixed.

6. Shape the salmon mixture into 8 thick patties: Scoop heaping mounds onto waxed paper or a plate, then tap them down a bit with a fork to flatten into thick disks. For best results, chill for 30 minutes, or up to overnight.

7. Heat the oil in a nonstick skillet over medium-high heat. Gently add the burgers. Fry until lightly browned on the bottom side, about 2 minutes. Flip and fry until crisp on the outside and still moist inside (burgers are best slightly undercooked), 1 to 2 minutes more. Serve on toasted mini-burger buns or rolls, with greens and Lime-Sesame Mayonnaise.

Seeded Honey Crisps

MAKES 24 TO 30 CRISPS

These quick, crispy snacks have nothing to do with nuts, except they remind me of why I like honey-roasted peanuts—they're slightly sweet and salty, with a satisfying crunch. These golden crisps make snappy cocktail fare by themselves, or serve them with Spicy Tunisian Sunset Dip (page 47).

You can whip these together in about fifteen minutes. For best results, mix the seed and sugar seasonings in separate bowls—when they're mixed all together in one bowl, the salt and sugar sink to the bottom, so it's harder to distribute the seasonings evenly. The egg wash mixture makes more than you'll need for this recipe, so if you're on a roll, you can bake up even more crisps with little extra effort. Excess crisps are never a problem: They disappear quickly, and they also make great gifts (store them airtight).

1 large egg white
1 teaspoon soy sauce
2 tablespoons honey
2 teaspoons sugar
½ teaspoon sea salt
¼ teaspoon ground white pepper
2 teaspoons cumin seed
2 teaspoons caraway seed
2 teaspoons white sesame seeds
   (or mixed with black seeds)
24 to 30 wonton wrappers
Nonstick vegetable oil spray

1. Arrange two racks in the upper third and lower third of the oven. Preheat the oven to 375°F. Line two 11×17-inch baking sheets with foil.

2. In a small bowl, beat together the egg white, soy sauce, and honey until thoroughly blended. Combine the sugar, salt, and white pepper in a small dish. Combine the cumin, caraway, and sesame seeds in a separate dish.

3. On each baking sheet, arrange as many wonton wrappers as will fit in a single layer. Spritz with nonstick spray until lightly coated. Turn the wrappers over. With a pastry brush, paint the egg mixture onto the wrappers. They should be generously coated. (Don't worry about being neat here—you can paint the whole tray, even in between the wontons.)

4. With your fingers, evenly sprinkle the sugar mixture over the wontons. Then sprinkle on the seed mixture.

5. Bake for 7 to 9 minutes, until golden and crisp, swapping and rotating the pans halfway through. Remove from the oven and let cool for 5 minutes on the baking sheet; the wontons will continue to crisp as they cool. Store airtight for up to 1 week.

NEW YORK'S TWENTIETH-CENTURY SOCIAL LIFE

When Prohibition arrived in 1919, an entire industry of entertainers, bartenders, cooks, and club owners prospered from the deep pockets and hedonistic pursuits of New York's Café Society. Admittedly, mobsters racked up most of the dough. But Prohibition was so vehemently opposed by almost everyone, that even the most respectable citizens partook of the alcohol-fueled underground without stigma. Their tastes created a lasting demand for ritzy evenings and entertainment, happening in places like these:

• **THE STORK CLUB.** When columnist Walter Winchell called The Stork Club "New York's New York-iest spot," the result was Oprah-like in its effect: He turned a failing club into an overnight, legendary success—one that, unlike other speakeasies, endured nearly four

decades, from 1929 to 1965. Owner Sherman Billingsley, a dirt-poor kid from Oklahoma and later a convicted bootlegger, gave his preferred customers his utmost attention, lavish gifts, and free food and drink, letting their plentiful fans and followers pay full price (a tactic later practiced at Studio 54). He also gave Winchell his own command post (table 51) and created the Cub Room as an inner chamber of gambling and drinking, restricted to the most exclusive clientele, including J. Edgar Hoover, Marilyn Monroe and Joe DiMaggio, the Duke and Duchess of Windsor, and in later years, Senator John F. Kennedy.

• **THE COTTON CLUB.** Picture this: It's 1929. Most of New York's show clubs are going dark, but for an energetic youth like you, the night is still young. You've got money and friends, and you're up for a night on the town. You and your "swells" pile into your Stutz Bearcat and head to Harlem's Jungle Alley—that is, of course, if you're white. The Cotton Club became the most famous of the Harlem nightclubs, but the only blacks allowed inside the club were performers and workers. Even interracial couples were turned away at the door. White mobsters owned the club, where Cab Calloway and Duke Ellington headlined. Lena Horne debuted in the club's sepia-toned chorus line, before Ethel Waters discovered she could sing. (If you're black, you might head instead to the Savoy, a jazz palace without a Jim Crow door policy.)

• **CAFE CARLYLE AND BEMELMANS BAR.** At "the Carlyle," Café Society partied on timelessly, marching through the decades into the twenty-first century, just to catch Bobby Short flash his million-dollar smile. For nearly thirty-seven years there, until his death in 2005, the black cabaret singer and pianist radiated the blithe spirit of Cole Porter, Billy "Take the A-Train" Strayhorn, Duke Ellington, and the Gershwins. His performances live on in his recordings, perfect for setting a clubby atmosphere at home. Next door to Cafe Carlyle, in the same building, Bemelmans Bar has been called "a rumpus room for sophisticated adults," due to of the playful murals by Ludwig Bemelmans, the man behind the *Madeline* series of children's books. Vintage bartenders in crisp uniforms pour classic cocktails, while customers nestled in black leather booths get joyfully lost just scanning the whimsical walls.

Hot Stuffed Dates

MAKES 12

The combination of dates with bacon and green olives may sound strange, but wait until you taste them. Sweet and salty are a compelling combination, and variations of this dish can be found in some of the classiest bars and restaurants coast to coast.

Los Angeles chef Suzanne Goin says 75 percent of her patrons order her specialty, Deglet Noor dates, which she fills with Parmesan nuggets, wraps in applewood smoked bacon, and roasts in a wood-burning oven. She reportedly describes them as "meat candy." When it comes to filling the dates, other chefs use Cabrales cheese, chèvre, or fromage blanc, merguez (Spanish paprika-lamb sausage), walnuts, almonds, or, as in this recipe, olives. Besides being simple to prepare, this version of stuffed dates may be assembled in advance and refrigerated up to two days, or frozen up to one month (no need to thaw; allow a few extra minutes to cook).

2 strips lean bacon
12 pitted dates
**12 small green olives, stuffed with
  pimientos**

1. Preheat the oven to 350°F. Cut each bacon strip into thirds. Then slice each third in half lengthwise, to form two narrow strips.

2. Stuff each date with an olive. Wrap a piece of bacon around each and secure with a toothpick. Repeat until a dozen dates are stuffed.

3. Place the dates on a baking sheet, evenly spaced. Bake for 20 to 25 minutes, turning halfway through, until the dates are hot and the bacon is crisp. If the bacon is not quite cooked, run the tray under the broiler until done. Serve right away, or keep warm.

Spicy Tunisian Sunset Dip

MAKES 1 CUP

Bright orange with carrots, and seasoned with warm spices, this tart-sweet dip can be served solo, or in tandem with hummus and other Mediterranean spreads. Seeded Honey Crisps (see recipe and photo of this dip on page 42) are ideal dippers, and pita chips and crudités work well, too.

2 teaspoons salt
2 teaspoons ground cumin
2 teaspoons sweet paprika
2 teaspoons ground coriander seed
1½ teaspoons powdered ginger
2 cloves garlic, chopped
6 ounces carrots (about 2 large)
3 tablespoons extra-virgin olive oil
3 tablespoons fresh lemon juice
2 teaspoons honey
1 teaspoon capers (preferably small)
⅛ teaspoon hot red pepper flakes, or to taste
1 tablespoon finely chopped parsley

1. Bring a pot of 1 quart water and salt to a boil. Measure the cumin, paprika, coriander, ginger, and garlic into a small bowl so they're ready to add later.

2. Cut the carrots into 1-inch chunks; halve the thicker chunks through the center so all the pieces will cook in about the same amount of time. When the water boils, add the carrots and simmer until a fork easily pokes through them, about 12 minutes. Drain.

3. In the same pot (still hot), heat the olive oil over medium heat. Add the cumin mixture and cook, stirring often, until the spices release their fragrance and lose their raw taste, about 2 minutes. Add the carrots and stir in the lemon juice and honey.

4. Scrape the carrot mixture, with all of the seasoned oil, into the work bowl of a food processor. Process until pureed. Scrape the dip into a bowl. Stir in the capers, red pepper flakes, and parsley. Serve slightly chilled or at room temperature. (The dip may be refrigerated up to 2 days; stir, taste, and refresh the seasonings as needed before serving.)

Tangerine Yakitori

MAKES 10 SKEWERS

Yakitori are tasty, Japanese skewered tidbits grilled over a charcoal fire. Chicken is one of the most popular versions, but the combinations can be as extreme as your imagination. The yakitori are first grilled partway through, then they're basted with a sauce and returned to the grill for another quick cooking, then basted in the sauce and returned to the grill to complete cooking. With the recipe below, feel free to include some mixed vegetables cut into two-inch lengths and skewered, such as green onion, red onion, eggplant, bell pepper, or mushrooms. (Note: To keep bamboo or wooden skewers from burning, soak them in water for thirty minutes first.)

3 tablespoons shiro miso ("white" miso, but it's actually a pale ochre)
2 tablespoons mirin (or honey)
3 tablespoons dry sherry
2 tablespoons sugar
½ cup tangerine juice
3 tablespoons lime juice
2 to 3 teaspoons chili-garlic sauce
1 pound boneless, skinless chicken thighs, cut into bite-size chunks
10 skewers
Nonstick cooking spray

1. Mix together the miso, mirin, sherry, sugar, and tangerine juice in a saucepan until smooth. Bring the mixture to a boil over medium-high heat, and boil, stirring occasionally, 10 to 15 minutes until reduced to ½ cup—watch to make sure the mixture doesn't boil over, and reduce the heat as needed. Let the mixture cool before using.

2. Combine the sauce mixture, lime juice, and chili-garlic sauce to taste. Marinate the chicken in the mixture, ideally for 5 hours, or between 2 hours and overnight.

3. When ready to cook, skewer the chicken pieces and let the excess marinade drain off. Fire up the grill. When the grill is very hot, spritz one side of each skewer with nonstick spray and place this side down on the grill. After this side gets nicely colored with grill marks, baste with the remaining marinade and flip the pieces over. Baste and flip several times during cooking, 5 to 7 minutes total. Serve hot or at room temperature.

Marinated Herb and Pepper Cheese

MAKES ABOUT ONE 6-OUNCE RAMEKIN OF CHEESE, PLUS OIL

I love having a jar of this robust, marinated soft cheese around for quick snacks and to jazz up other recipes. The oil itself is a culinary treat and can be used wherever a fruity, herb-infused olive oil is called for. This recipe blends feta cheese with cream cheese, then marinates them in fruity olive oil and fresh herbs. It's kind of like a less expensive alternative to marinated buffalo mozzarella or goat cheese, but it's delicious in itself and provides a comparable tart and pungent flavor.

What can you do with this marinated cheese? Dot nuggets of it on flavorful greens, using the olive oil to make a vinaigrette. Or, serve the cheese with toasted crostini and sun-dried tomatoes. Melt the cheese with a bit of cream and use it as a spunky herbed cream sauce. Once you have it on hand, you'll find a zillion uses for this zesty cheese and oil combo.

1 clove garlic
2 ounces cream cheese
2 to 3 ounces feta cheese
½ teaspoon coarsely ground black pepper
2 sprigs fresh herbs, such as rosemary, lemon thyme, or marjoram
¾ to 1 cup extra virgin olive oil

1. Chop the garlic clove by dropping it into a food processor with the blade running. Add the cheeses and thoroughly blend to form a smooth paste. Add the pepper and pulse to combine. Line a mold, such as a 6-ounce ramekin or a small cup, with plastic wrap. With a spatula, spoon the cheese mixture into the lined mold and bring up the sides of the plastic to enclose fully. Twist the ends together and close off with a twist-tie. Refrigerate until firm (about 2 hours).

2. Select a squat, wide-mouthed jar or other container, one large enough to hold at least 1½ cups. Drop the fresh herbs into the jar. Pour in the olive oil. Remove the cheese from the mold, cut it into small pieces, and drop the pieces into the container. Spoon the oil over the pieces to coat them thoroughly. Seal the jar and refrigerate for at least 1 hour, preferably overnight, before using. As long as the cheese is submerged in the oil (you can add more oil if necessary), the mixture will keep 1 week refrigerated.

Chèvre-Stuffed Cornbread Kisses

MAKES 24 MINI-MUFFINS

These tiny, golden cornbread muffins may look traditional, but they're filled with a tangy white cloud of goat cheese and cream cheese, enhanced by chives. Fill greased mini-muffin tins (with muffins 1¾ to 2 inches in diameter, twelve muffins per tin) directly with the batter; the crust is better when they're baked in the muffin tin rather than in paper liners.

3 ounces goat cheese
3 ounces cream cheese with chives
1 cup yellow cornmeal
1 cup all purpose flour
⅓ cup granulated sugar
1 tablespoon baking powder
1 teaspoon salt
1 cup buttermilk
⅓ cup vegetable oil
1 large egg

1. Preheat the oven to 375°F. Generously grease 2 mini-muffin tins.

2. In a small bowl, blend together the goat cheese and cream cheese with a fork.

3. Combine the cornmeal, flour, sugar, baking powder, and salt in a mixing bowl. Measure the buttermilk and oil into a measuring cup and add the egg. Beat lightly with a fork until blended. Pour the liquid ingredients into the dry ingredients. Mix just until blended.

4. Fill the muffin cups about half full. Spoon a lump of the cheese mixture into each muffin. Top each muffin with the remaining batter—it's okay if some of the cheese pokes through the batter. Bake about 15 minutes, or until the edges are golden brown. Let the muffins cool in the pans about 10 minutes before removing. Serve warm or at room temperature.

MIXING THE SALAD AT STUDIO 54

The pinnacle of disco madness arrived in New York City on April 26, 1977, in the form of Studio 54. Food was never the attraction at Studio 54, especially for the cocaine-sniffing clientele; superstardom, in an unrelenting party atmosphere, was. The decade's most famous faces, from Andy Warhol to Muhammad Ali, Liza to Cher, the Trumps to the McCartneys, made Studio 54 one of the most legendary nightspots on earth.

Co-founder Steve Rubell imperiously guarded the entry, seeking out the beautiful nobodies, blacks, whites, and exotic mixed-breeds, gays and straights, to balance the heavyweights of stardom. It was what he called "mixing the salad." He and his partner, Ian Schrager, understood that exclusivity could be created. They poured out lavish gifts to celebrities, far beyond alcohol and drugs, knowing that if the celebs came, so would the "little people"—the ones who actually paid for their drinks.

Studio 54's heyday ended spectacularly in 1979. Under the watchful eye of the man-in-the-moon (which hung over the dance floor and lit up when a large coke spoon was suspended under its nose), federal agents discovered garbage bags full of cash and ledgers detailing every gift the owners had ever bestowed, including drugs and poppers (amyl nitrate). Rubell and Schrager were jailed for tax evasion, and the club is now reincarnated at Las Vegas's MGM Grand, complete with disco moon and spoon (though they're not displayed together).

Martini-Butter Steak with Cocktail Onions and Caperberries

SERVES 4 AS BITE-SIZE BAR BITES

"I am prepared to believe that a dry martini slightly impairs the palate, but think what it does for the soul"—and the steak! Alec Waugh, novelist and gastronome, not only paid homage to the martini, he reportedly created the cocktail party itself. But what's a party without food? This martini-inspired steak features caperberries, which look like giant capers, and are the enormous, near-ready-to-flower-buds of the caper plant. Almond-sized and dark green with long stems, they're quite festive to look at, and extremely tart. A whole one musters immediate mouth puckering, but they're just right for nibbling with cocktails. Here, they're chopped up with another pickled favorite, cocktail onions, and mixed to create a compound butter flavored with gin and vermouth. Look for caperberries in jars at specialty markets or in bulk at olive bars. Capers may be substituted.

2 tablespoons gin
2 tablespoons dry vermouth
2 tablespoons cold butter, in one chunk
1 tablespoon chopped cocktail onions, plus extra for garnish
1 tablespoon chopped caperberries, plus extra for garnish
Two 1-inch-thick steaks (such as New York strip steaks), about 1 pound total
Olive oil
Salt and fresh coarsely ground black pepper

1. Heat the gin and vermouth in a small skillet or saucepan over medium heat until the alcohol burns off and the mixture reduces by half, 1 to 2 minutes. (This takes the harshness out but leaves the flavors in. Be careful when heating liquor; it may flame, which is another way of burning off the alcohol and creates quite a pyrotechnic effect, but don't let things get out of control. Keep a pot lid handy for smothering if the flames get too high.)

2. Spear the butter chunk on the tines of a fork and slowly stir into the liquid until the butter is incorporated. Stir in the onions and caperberries. Pour the mixture into a small container and chill until solid.

(continued)

55

3. Lightly coat the steaks with olive oil, then season with salt and pepper. Heat a skillet or grill pan over medium-high heat until very hot. (You may also grill or broil the steaks.) Sear the steaks on both sides, flipping halfway through, about 5 minutes total time for rare and 10 minutes for medium. Top each steak with a lump of Martini Butter, spreading it over the steak as it melts. Let the steaks rest 5 to 10 minutes. Slice into bite-size pieces. Scatter the pieces on a tray with whole cocktail onions and caperberries, and serve with cocktail picks.

THE PUMP ROOM'S CELEBRITY PLAYLIST

The Pump Room opened in Chicago's Ambassador Hotel East in 1938, immediately serving socialites and celebrities such as John Barrymore, little Liza Minnelli and mom Judy Garland, and newlyweds Lauren Bacall and Humphrey Bogart. Through the years, famous diners have included Robert Redford and Paul Newman (who lunched on ham sandwiches and pilsners while filming *The Sting*), Mick Jagger (who held a private party there), and sports legends Muhammad Ali and Michael Jordan, among others. And, before he became super-famous, musician Phil Collins was turned away at the door—for not wearing a jacket.

The incident goes like this: former Led Zeppelin frontman Robert Plant and Collins are staying at the hotel, and cruise down to the Pump Room for a drink. Apparently the black leather jacket Collins wears doesn't meet the dress code, but Plant's loud checkered suit does. Collins is turned away, and tells the story repeatedly on late-night television. Eventually, the Pump Room management, in an act of contrition seasoned with a sense of humor, sends him a paint-spattered jacket and note saying he is indeed welcome anytime. Collins named an album after the escapade, entitled *No Jacket Required*, which won the 1985 Grammy for Pop Album of the Year.

WINE BAR AND BISTRO PLATES

W hat would wine be without food? Especially savory snacks and small plates, the kind served at enotecas, wine bars, and European bistros . . .

Relax the mind and mellow out. Pull up a chair at a sidewalk cafe and people-watch (everyday people can be just as interesting as celebrities). Or visit a vineyard and watch the grapes grow, knowing that one day they'll be splashed into the same glass you now hold in your hand.

From tapas to *cichetti*, nibbles to light meals, these foods taste best with wine, by the glass, bottle, or simple carafe. Savor them with vintage cabernet, chilled *junmai* sake, or oloroso sherry. This is your golden leisure time, where every moment and every taste counts, and nothing is more important than the daydream you're in right now.

Cichetti Olives and Garlic

SERVES 6 TO 8 AS BAR BITES

Fried olives appear as bar snacks, known collectively as cichetti, in Venetian wine bars (see the sidebar on page 63). Though they're not traditional, I also like to fry up a batch of pickled garlic cloves, which are tart but not as salty as olives, and pickled cocktail onions, too.

With so many varieties of olives available, it's easy to get creative. Smaller olives need less oil for frying, and they fry quicker than large olives. Small olives can be popped in the mouth whole, while large, meaty ones generally require two bites. Each has its sensory advantages, so take your pick.

Olives stuffed with lemon are a fitting complement to martinis. Some people get fancy, filling the olives with cheese, almonds, or sausage before breading and frying.

About 36 pitted green olives, plain or stuffed, drained
About 24 pickled garlic cloves (or cocktail onions), drained (optional)
⅓ cup all-purpose flour
1 large egg, beaten
⅓ cup plain or seasoned dry breadcrumbs
Vegetable oil for deep-frying

In Spain, fried olives are served with a side of Romesco sauce, which blends red peppers, tomato, and almonds with wine vinegar, and adds a sweet complement to the saltiness of the olives. But start with this simple recipe and after that, let inspiration be your guide.

1. Working with several pieces at a time, roll the olives (and garlic or onions if using) in the flour, then in the egg, and then in the breadcrumbs. (Shallow plastic food-storage containers work great for coating each ingredient; just seal and gently shake.) At this point, you may refrigerate the coated pieces in a single layer, without touching, up to 1 day before frying.

2. Heat about 1 inch of oil in a pot, pan, or wok for deep-frying. When a small cube of bread fries up toasty brown in 30 seconds, the oil is ready (about 375°F). Fry the olives (and garlic and onions) rolling them in the oil for even browning, until golden and crisp, 1½ to 2 minutes—be careful: oil may splatter.

3. With a slotted spoon, scoop out the pieces and drain on paper towels. Serve hot, or let the cichetti rest at room temperature up to 4 hours, or refrigerated for up to 2 days. Reheat in a 300°F oven until warm, about 5 minutes.

Wild About Harry's Croque Monsieur

MAKES 2 SANDWICHES

The Croque Monsieur may be French in name, but an Italian turned it into classic bar food. Harry's Bar in Venice is famous for the Bellini, a Prosecco (Italian "champagne") and peach juice cocktail, and for their toasted cheese finger sandwich, wrapped in a pristine white paper napkin. Sandwiches are, according to owner Arrigo Cipriani in *The Harry's Bar Cookbook*, "the ideal bar food—light, easy to eat, not too expensive."

When it comes to cooking, the fewer the ingredients, the more important their selection. This version has a few of its own flavor tweaks, but like the Harry's Bar version, it's made with a Swiss-style cheese, not a Cheddar or provolone. And to make a truly extraordinary Croque Monsieur, I believe Gruyère is essential. Most other Swiss cheeses just don't pack the same rich, nutty flavor as Gruyère, though they'll still taste good in a pinch.

A classic Harry's Bar Croque Monsieur is served crustless on unsweetened, homemade, white sandwich bread, the kind sold at good bakeries, or made by Pepperidge Farm. But this mixture tastes great on all types of bread. By the way, wrapping the sandwiches in little white napkins is more than cosmetic: they absorb the oil, keep fingers clean, and help retain the heat.

4 ounces Gruyère cheese, shredded
1½ teaspoons white wine
    Worcestershire sauce (or regular)
½ teaspoon Dijon mustard
1 teaspoon good-quality mayonnaise
Dash white pepper
4 slices white bread, crusts removed,
    if desired
4 slices (3 ounces) sliced ham (boiled
    or black forest style)
1 tablespoon olive oil for frying

1. Mash together the cheese, Worcestershire, mustard, mayonnaise, and white pepper.

2. Spread the cheese mixture over one side of each of the bread slices. Top two slices of bread with the ham, then flip the remaining bread slices, cheese side down, onto the ham. Press down on the each sandwich with a large spatula to help them hold together.

(continued)

61

3. Measure the olive oil into a large skillet. Dipping into the oil, generously brush one side of the sandwiches with oil. Heat the skillet or griddle over medium to medium-high heat. When the pan and oil are hot, add the sandwiches with the oiled side facing up. When the bottom side is crisp and golden, after 3 to 4 minutes, flip the sandwiches over and fry the other side, also until crisp and golden, for another 3 to 4 minutes, peeking to make sure they don't burn.

4. Slice the sandwiches in half lengthwise. For the Harry's Bar effect, wrap white paper napkins neatly around the bottom halves, and serve hot.

VENETIAN CHIC: CICHETTI, BACARI, AND OMBRA

Throughout Italy, you can drink at enoteche and osterie, but the bacaro is a type of bar unique to Venezia, and so are the bar snacks served there, known as cichetti.

Cichetti are often described as Venetian tapas, Spain's small dishes. As a trade hub, Venice developed a love of exotic spices and tasty little snacks from the Moors, as did Spain. Cichetti can be fried olives (page 58), toothpick-speared mortadella and fontina, marinated vegetables, or a polpetti (meatball) on crisp polenta. But being a city on the sea, Venice specializes in seafood-based cichetti.

The bacaro is more rustic or casual than other Italian bars. Patrons typically eat standing up, at a long counter, sipping on ombra, a glass of the house wine, or something fancier, like a sparkling local Prosecco. The word ombra means "shadow" and explanations of its origin vary (naturally). Author Giuliano Hazan says the interpretation he's heard relates to meeting in the "ombra" of the bell tower at St. Mark's Square. Others agree, with varying details: one version says wine vendors moved their carts into the tower's shade as the sun shifted; another says people would sip wine at tables in the shade. A more romantic account describes "ombras" as the shady places where gondoliers parked their boats and took breaks from the sun, sipping wine with their colleagues, and which evolved into the informal cichetti bars, the bacari, we know today.

A bacaro swells at midday and early evening. Locals jam together to discuss the day's news, gossip, visit, and nibble on the inexpensive cichetti—which may also be spelled cicheti or cicchetti. All are pronounced as chee-KEHT-tee, but according to Giuliano Hazan: "Venetians seem to have an aversion to double consonants, and any Italian word that has a double consonant loses one in the Venetian dialect equivalent. So, in standard Italian, the spelling would be cicchetti but a Venetian is probably more likely to spell it cicheti." Or cichetti, which is, as yet another spelling variation, as delightfully capricious as Italia herself.

ENOTECA, PLURAL: ENOTECHE

Most people think of the enoteca, or Italian wine bar, as a place to enjoy wine by the glass, with a light meal or snack on the side. But an Italian enoteca can offer more, or fewer, services than this.

Some enoteche simply sell bottles of wine and send you on your way, kind of like your neighborhood liquor store. (One traveler described a particular enoteca as a place where old men get their wine.) In some cases, though, the state and the local winery consortium band together to sponsor a more impressive enoteca, showcasing regional wines by bottle and glass. The enoteche most revered by travelers are those with compact tables and food—usually small plates and little bites—to complement the wine and vice versa. A few enoteche operate their own full-scale restaurants, where the wines may be enjoyed over a multi-course meal, from glorious antipasti to decadent dolci (desserts).

Teacup Tomato Toasts

SERVES 6 AS BAR BITES

Miniature tomatoes, about the size of dimes, arrive in summer at farmers' markets and specialty stores. They're lusciously sweet, and even smaller than teardrop, grape, or cherry tomatoes, but those types may be used in a pinch. Here, miniature tomatoes are cooked whole, cupped in scooped-out pieces of French bread, seasoned with olive oil, sea salt, and balsamic vinegar. If you substitute grape or cherry tomatoes, use the smallest ones you can find (or halve them). This is an ideal recipe for showing off your ultra-sexy specialty oils, vinegars, sea salts, and fresh herbs. Besides olive oil, try macadamia oil flavored with lemon myrtle (from Australia), basil or rosemary flavored oil, orange or lemon olive oil, or walnut oil. Vinegars should be mildly acidic, like balsamic (red or white) or a French Banyuls. You can also bake the tomatoes with minced garlic or shallot, fresh herbs, grated Parmesan or Romano, or goat cheese crumbles. By the way, this dish is perfect toaster-oven fare.

One small (6- to 8-ounce) loaf French or Italian bread (or half of a long 1 pound loaf)
8 to 10 ounces miniature tomatoes (or small teardrop, grape, or cherry tomatoes)
3 to 4 tablespoons extra virgin olive oil, or other flavorful oil
Sea salt to taste
Freshly ground black pepper to taste
2 to 3 tablespoons balsamic vinegar
Julienned fresh basil for garnish (optional)

1. Preheat the oven to 300°F.

2. Slice the bread in half lengthwise (as if making a sandwich), then reassemble the top and bottom together. Cut the loaf into three pieces, each 3 to 4 inches long. Pluck out the soft centers of each piece, leaving a cavity or cup to hold the tomatoes. Arrange the bread on a baking sheet, cavity-side up.

3. Place a handful of tomatoes in each cavity. Sprinkle the olive oil, salt, and pepper over the tomatoes and surrounding surface of the bread. Bake for 30 to 40 minutes, until the tomatoes are soft and the bread toasted. Drizzle the vinegar on top, and add basil, if desired. The tomatoes will be very hot inside. Let cool for a few minutes, then serve. Eat the toasts with your hands, and provide toothpicks for stabbing at any tomato escapees that fall off the toasts as you eat them.

Bresaola Carpaccio with Parmesan, Capers, and Basil Oil

SERVES 4 AS BAR BITES

One day at Harry's Bar in Venice, as the legend goes, a contessa who was a longtime patron told owner Giuseppe Cipriani she was on doctor's orders to avoid cooked meat. Minutes later, Cipriani emerged from the kitchen with a platter of ultra-thin-sliced raw beef, dressed simply with olive oil, lemon juice, and a few shards of shaved cheese. The meat was a stunning red, as brilliant as the crimson hues in the Renaissance paintings of Vittore Carpaccio, and a classic dish was born.

Since that day in 1950, chefs have put a trendy "carpaccio" tag on almost any thinly sliced food on a platter, including zucchini, tuna, and tomatoes. Here, air-cured beef known as bresaola stands in brilliantly for the raw meat, paying homage to the original without overstretching the concept. Any delicatessen that carries Italian meats beyond salami and prosciutto should stock bresaola.

¼ pound thinly sliced bresaola
1 whole lemon
4 teaspoons basil-flavored olive oil
1 tablespoon capers
1 ounce cheese shavings (Parmigiano-Reggiano, Grana Padano, or Asiago)
Freshly ground pepper (preferably mixed peppercorns)

1. Arrange the bresaola slices on a plate, overlapping them slightly.

2. Shred the zest from half the lemon over the bresaola. Squeeze 2 teaspoons lemon juice into a small bowl. Add the olive oil and stir to combine. Sprinkle the capers and cheese shavings over the bresaola. Spoon the lemon-oil mixture over the bresaola, and top with a generous grating of pepper. Serve at room temperature.

YOU SAY SALUMI, I SAY SALAMI...

A good Italian deli (a salumeria in Italy, which means "cured meat shop") can seduce and nearly overwhelm the senses—long batons of garlicky salami; short, plump, smoky sausages; rolls of pepper-encrusted, fat-streaked pancetta; rosy slices of aromatic prosciutto; vats of oil- and brine-cured olives; pungent, vinegary salads; and cheeses ranging from wagon wheel–sized rounds to perky little pigs, complete with curled tail and floppy ears.

Watch your vowels here: Salami is the plural form of salame, which is a single cured sausage, as defined below. Salumi is the comprehensive term for all cured meats, derived from "salare," which means to salt, and they can be smoky and sweet or hot and spicy. Here are some of the salumi items commonly found in Italian markets:

• **BRESAOLA**—This is air-dried, salted beef, dark and dense, similar to Swiss Bundner Fleisch but more tender: it almost melts in your mouth. Usually it is sliced thin and served with lemon and olive oil. (See page 66 for Bresaola Carpaccio with Parmesan, Capers, and Basil Oil.)

• **CAPPACOLA**—This spiced, cured pork shoulder can be hot with red pepper or sweet and mild with sugar and white wine. It has various spellings, including cappicola and capocollo.

• **COPPA**—This salame of boiled pork is spiced with pepper, nutmeg, and orange peel.

• **MORTADELLA**—This is the product on which Oscar Mayer bologna was based, though mortadella is much more than kid stuff. This finely ground pork sausage from Bologna comes in different grades and variations, some studded with pistachios, coriander seeds, or peppercorns, and often wonderfully garlicky. Others include a pinch of cinnamon or nutmeg. Mortadella is buttery, subtle, and well seasoned, but not spicy like salami.

• **PANCETTA**—This Italian pork belly is similar to bacon but different in that it's not smoked. Pancetta is sold as a slab or rolled into a cylinder. It's the meat of choice for true Spaghetti alla Carbonara.

• **PROSCIUTTO CRUDO**—Most Americans are familiar with this exquisite dry cured ham, served thinly sliced with melon or figs, or wrapped around Italian breadsticks (grissini). Prosciutto di Parma is perhaps the most popular, praised for its salty yet distinctive taste. My favorite is actually Prosciutto di San Daniele, which is a bit sweeter and more delicate in flavor. From the Friuli region, the San Daniele prosciutto is salted for less time than the Parma version, and it's pressed to distribute the fat around the ham. Prosciutto cotto is cooked ham, similar to our boiled ham, and entirely different from prosciutto crudo.

• **SALAME**—Dozens of regional "salami" exist, but all are dried meats (pork or beef primarily), coarsely or finely ground with a mix of lean and fat, garlic (usually), pepper, herbs, and sometimes wine. They're dried in a heated chamber, then moved to cold storage to cure. Generally speaking, spicier salami is made in the south, while northern Italy produces milder versions.

• **SOPPRESSATA**—This air-dried, coarsely ground pork sausage currently ranks high on the trendy food barometer, due to its balanced spices, flexible texture, and rustic look. It comes sweet or hot, and often stands in for prosciutto.

Home-style Salmon "L'Ermitage"

MAKES 1¾ CUPS

Because he couldn't find any smoked salmon of quality in Los Angeles, Chef Michel Blanchet began curing and herb-smoking his own Norwegian salmon at L'Ermitage Restaurant, circa 1975. The results were stunning, and he now supplies a variety of smoked fish to area restaurants and gourmet shops. But not everyone lives in Southern California. Not a problem. Even regular salmon tastes great in this home-style rendition of a Blanchet classic. It calls for cold-smoked salmon (like lox) and hot or wood smoked salmon (the firm, dry kind), mixed with the same seasonings found in Chef Blanchet's Smoked Salmon Tartar. Both types of salmon typically come in four-ounce packages, which will last unopened in the fridge until their use-by date, generally several weeks. Serve this with toast points (page 18), or Gougère (page 21).

4 ounces wood-smoked salmon, preferably oak-smoked
4 ounces cold smoked salmon, like lox
3 tablespoons sour cream
2 tablespoons fresh lemon juice
2 tablespoons chopped sweet onion (like Maui or Vidalia), or red onion
2 tablespoons capers, chopped
1 tablespoon finely chopped fresh parsley

1. Remove and discard the skin from the wood-smoked salmon. Chop both salmons into small bits.

2. Combine the salmon with the remaining ingredients. The mixture should be light and somewhat loose (not packed).

Serve mildly chilled or at room temperature with toasts, crackers, or Gougère. The mixture will keep refrigerated for up to 2 days.

Fig and Balsamic Pork Tenderloin on Walnut-Arugula Salad

SERVES 4 AS A SMALL PLATE

In the mood for the sort of small but elegant plates served in wine country? This dish will have you dreaming of vineyards and lazy days in the sun. You can cook the pork and fig sauce a day in advance, then assemble the salad right before eating.

1 pound whole pork tenderloin, rinsed
  and patted dry
1 tablespoon lemon-pepper seasoning salt
1 tablespoon olive oil
About 15 dried mission figs, tough stems
  removed
¼ cup balsamic vinegar
¼ cup water
5 ounces arugula
2 tablespoons walnut oil (or other
  flavorful oil)
⅓ cup walnut pieces

1. Cut the tenderloin in half, to make 2 short, plump pieces. Measure the lemon-pepper salt onto a plate and roll the pork tenderloin in it to coat all sides. Heat the olive oil in a heavy nonstick skillet over medium-high heat. Add the tenderloin pieces and quickly brown on all sides, about 5 minutes total.

2. While the pork browns, combine the figs, balsamic vinegar, and water. When the pork has browned, remove the pan from the heat and carefully pour the fig mixture over the pork and into the pan. Cover and braise at a low simmer over medium-low heat, turning the pieces halfway through, until the pork registers 150°F and the pork is slightly pink inside, about 15 minutes.

3. Remove the tenderloin from the pan and let it rest a few minutes before slicing. Cover the pan and remove it from the heat to conserve the pan juices. The sauce should be slightly thick; if it's too watery, cook uncovered until it resembles a thin glaze; if too thick, stir in a spoonful of water. (If preparing the dish in advance, refrigerate the juices and figs separately from the pork. Bring both to room temperature before serving.)

4. While the pork rests, toss the arugula with the walnut oil and set it out on a serving platter or individual plates. Slice the pork into thin pieces and arrange on the arugula. Spoon the figs and pan juices on top. Sprinkle on the walnuts, and serve.

Prosciutto-Mascarpone Pinwheels

SERVES 4 AS BAR BITES

Packaged prosciutto makes classy bar food spontaneously feasible, as in this simple and attractive recipe. Most supermarkets carry pre-sliced packages in their deli sections. For this dish, don't even bother to separate the slices, as they're already shingled and overlapping to form a single "sheet." Of course, freshly sliced prosciutto can taste even better, but don't slice it too thin or it will be hard to work with.

6 ounces mascarpone cheese
3 ounces sliced prosciutto (about 10 slices)
1 bunch fresh basil leaves (about 30 leaves)
Small breads, crackers, or melon slices
(optional), for serving

1. Bring the mascarpone to room temperature so it's easy to spread. Spread out a length of plastic wrap, about 16 inches long. Shingle the slices of prosciutto across the plastic wrap so they overlap slightly, forming an 8- or 9-inch square. Note that you'll have two sides that are shingled, and two that are clean and even. (If the prosciutto is paper-thin, you may need to patch it together in places, which is fine. You just want to create a single solid "sheet" of prosciutto.)

2. Spread the mascarpone over the prosciutto, leaving a half-inch border on one of the even edges. (You may find that patting it out with your fingers is easier than spreading it.)

3. Arrange the basil leaves in a single layer over the mascarpone. Roll the prosciutto up and over the filling, jelly-roll fashion, rolling toward the edge that has no filling. Tightly wrap the plastic around the log, twisting the ends shut. Chill until firm. Slice into rounds about 1/3 inch thick. Serve with crackers, crostini, or melon, or just eat the pinwheels plain, as finger food. The roll may be made a day in advance and sliced just before serving.

Puff Pastry Pizza Squares with Balsamic Duxelles

SERVES 3 AS BAR BITES

Duxelles is essentially finely chopped mushrooms, sautéed until they lose their liquid and reduce down to a coarse spread—simple, but effective. This recipe brightens the traditional duxelle treatment with balsamic vinegar and soy sauce. Cook the duxelles in advance, if you wish. Then, with sun-dried tomato pesto in the pantry, a box of puff pastry in the freezer, and a wedge of Brie in the fridge, voilà! You've got delicate, flaky pizza bites whenever the mood hits.

2 tablespoons butter
2 tablespoons minced shallot or onion
2 large cloves garlic, minced (about 1 tablespoon)
6 ounces finely chopped portobello mushrooms
1 teaspoon soy sauce
2 teaspoons balsamic vinegar
Salt to taste
1 sheet frozen puff pastry
3 tablespoons prepared sun-dried tomato pesto
3 to 4 ounces Brie, rind removed
1 scallion, chopped (both green and white parts)

1. Melt the butter in a skillet over medium heat. Add the shallot and garlic and cook, stirring often, until softened, about 3 minutes. Add the mushrooms and cook, stirring, until the mushrooms release their juices and most of the liquid evaporates, about 8 minutes. Stir in the soy sauce and vinegar and continue cooking until the liquid is absorbed, another 2 minutes or so. Add salt to taste. (The duxelles may be refrigerated up to 1 week or frozen up to 2 months; bring to room temperature before using.)

2. Thaw the puff pastry according to manufacturer's directions (usually 30 minutes). Preheat the oven to 400°F.

3. Unfold the pastry sheet. Slice through the folds and across the sheet, cutting the pastry into 9 squares. Arrange the pastry pieces on an ungreased baking sheet. On each piece, smear some tomato pesto, then top with duxelles, followed by a lump of Brie, and sprinkle with scallions.

4. Bake 15 to 18 minutes, until the pastry puffs and browns and the cheese melts. Let the pastries rest a few minutes, then serve hot or at room temperature.

Eggplant Pizzettes

SERVES 4 TO 6 AS BAR BITES

Eggplant rounds serve here as mini-pizzas, flavored with the smoky, sweet undertones of barbecue sauce, balsamic vinegar, and sun-dried tomatoes. Pecan bits, toasted on a blanket of melting cheese, add a satisfying, crunchy bite. For a breadlike complement, serve with long, thin grissini (Italian breadsticks) stuck in a tall, narrow glass.

⅓ cup chopped dry-packed sun-dried tomatoes
¼ cup barbecue sauce (see Headnote)
3 tablespoons balsamic vinegar
1 eggplant (about 1¼ pounds)
¼ cup basil oil or extra-virgin olive oil
8 ounces sliced smoked provolone
3 tablespoons finely chopped shallot or red
   onion
¼ cup finely chopped pecan pieces
Chopped fresh mint or basil for garnish
   (optional)

Use a barbecue sauce on the sweet and smoky side (I prefer Stubb's Smokey Mesquite Bar-B-Q Sauce). If you use oil-packed sun-dried tomatoes instead of dry-packed ones, you can skip microwaving the sauce to reconstitute the tomatoes.

1. Preheat the broiler. Line a baking sheet with foil and lightly spritz with nonstick spray.

2. Stir together the tomatoes, barbecue sauce, and vinegar in a microwave-safe container. Partially cover (to prevent splattering) and microwave on High 60 seconds, stirring halfway through, to soften the tomatoes.

3. Slice the eggplant into ½-inch-thick rounds. Arrange the slices in a single layer on the baking sheet. Brush the oil on both sides of each slice. Broil 5 to 6 inches from the heat for 5 to 7 minutes, until the pieces start to brown. Flip the rounds over and broil another 5 to 7 minutes, until the pieces are mostly cooked through and easily pierced with a fork, but not mushy.

4. Smear a bit of the sauce on each slice. Cover with the cheese, casually tearing the slices with your fingers to fit (pieces can overlap). Sprinkle the shallot over the cheese and top with the pecan pieces.

5. Broil for 3 to 5 minutes more, until the cheese softens and gently melts (watch closely so the pecans don't burn). If desired, garnish with fresh mint or basil, and serve.

Bursting Tomato Gratin

SERVES 4 AS BAR BITES

Besides being packed with flavor, luscious little cherry, grape, or teardrop tomatoes make this gratin a breeze. They're cooked whole, requiring no chopping, nestled under a creamy layer of goat cheese and herbs and a crunchy breadcrumb topping. When you bite into the gratin, these tender tomatoes literally burst with flavor: they pop in your mouth, letting their sweet juices mingle with the tangy cheese and herbs.

The gratin may be made earlier in the day and served at room temperature, or reheated. You can also prepare the creamy cheese mixture a day in advance; then on serving day, simply pour the tomatoes into a glass baking dish with some olive oil, cover with the cheese mixture and bread-crumbs, and bake, slice, and serve. Voilà! Elegant little bar plates for very little effort.

1 large egg
⅓ cup cream
1 tablespoon all-purpose flour
5 ounces soft goat cheese, plain or garlic and herb seasoned
1½ tablespoons fresh rosemary leaves, chopped (omit if using basil below)
¼ teaspoon freshly ground black pepper, or to taste
2 tablespoons extra-virgin olive oil
1 pound mini-tomatoes, such as grape, teardrop, or cherry tomatoes
½ cup chopped fresh basil (omit if using rosemary above)
¼ cup fine dried breadcrumbs, preferably garlic-herb seasoned
2 tablespoons freshly grated Parmesan or Romano cheese
1 clove garlic, minced
About ¼ teaspoon salt, or to taste
Freshly ground black pepper

1. Preheat the oven to 425°F.

2. In a small mixing bowl, beat the egg until mixed. Beat in the cream and flour. Mash in the goat cheese, rosemary, if using, and pepper, until the mixture is well combined and creamy. If the mixture is too thick, blend in more cream: the mixture should be moist and easily spreadable, like a cream cheese frosting. (This can be made a day in advance and refrigerated.)

3. Pour 1 tablespoon olive oil into a shallow baking dish just big enough to hold the tomatoes in a single layer (a ceramic tart pan or glass pie pan works best). Add the tomatoes, rolling them around so the oil coats them as well as the bottom and sides of the dish. Stir in the basil, if using. (You can prepare this step earlier in the day, but chop and add the basil just before cooking.)

4. Mix together the breadcrumbs, Parmesan or Romano, garlic, salt, and pepper to taste. Sprinkle half of this mixture on the tomatoes.

5. Gently spoon the goat cheese mixture over the tomatoes and crumbs, distributing it evenly. Top with the remaining breadcrumb mixture and drizzle the remaining tablespoon of olive oil on top.

6. Bake until the tomatoes soften but have not yet burst, 15 to 18 minutes. The top should be golden brown, but if not, finish the gratin under the broiler for a few seconds. Slice the gratin into wedges and serve hot or at room temperature, with small forks (or reheat in a 375°F oven for about 5 minutes).

ENRICO'S: SAN FRANCISCO'S "STREET FOOD"

Enrico's, San Francisco's landmark club in the North Beach neighborhood, became the first Parisian-style outdoor café in the Bay Area in 1958. For half a century, a broad clientele of bohemians, glitterati, politicians, and socialites amused themselves on its heated patio. Tourists and locals alike sipped and slurped, mesmerized by the surrounding street scene: the gaudy Broadway strip that teems with neon lights, urban adrenaline, and sexy naughtiness. Bankrupt and closed for four years in the '80s, Enrico's charged back with veteran and newly minted bartenders mixing Manhattans and mojitos, and serving fried olives, pizza margherita, and smoked-salmon bruschetta. Sadly, over time, even the large planters, romantic candles, and cool jazz couldn't insulate the avant-garde institution from rising crime and rowdy crowds. In 2006, lacking a favorable lease renewal, Enrico's shut its doors permanently, though you can still get a glimpse of it in the 1968 film *Bullitt* as the site where Steve McQueen meets his informant Eddie.

Grilled Pepper Gondolas

SERVES 2 OR 3 AS BAR BITES

When sweet bell peppers are sliced along their contours, the sections make excellent "boats" for holding melted cheese and other toppings. You could call them canoes, I suppose, but with Italian ingredients, gondolas seems more appropriate.

They're especially tasty grilled, indoors or out, to char the pepper skins, but broiling creates a tasty dish, too. Either way, the peppers soften but remain al dente, warm but slightly crisp, a wonderful texture. They're topped with olive oil, a blast of black pepper, and pungent anchovy fillets (if you're anti-anchovy, leave them off or add sliced olives). This recipe calls for one pepper, but it's just as easy to make two or three at the same time.

1 red bell pepper (or other color)
1 tablespoon extra-virgin olive oil
3 ounces sliced smoked provolone
Freshly ground black pepper
3 to 6 anchovy fillets, packed in oil
1 tablespoon minced fresh parsley

1. Preheat an indoor gas or electric grill, or an outdoor grill, until hot. (For a charcoal grill, when the coals are ashed over, rake or spread them out so the food can cook directly over the coals. For a gas grill, fire up the burners so the food cooks directly over the heat.)

2. All bell peppers are shaped differently, but the goal is to end up with concave or boat-shaped pieces that can hold other ingredients. Cut the bell pepper lengthwise along the natural contours into 3 or 4 wide pieces, or about 6 slender ones. Discard the core, seeds, and membrane.

3. Brush the olive oil on both sides of each pepper slice or "gondola," then nest 2 layers of sliced cheese on the inside, trimming to fit. Top with a generous amount of pepper and a half or whole anchovy fillet. Grill the gondolas, cheese-side up, over direct heat, covered or tented with foil, until the peppers are lightly cooked but still firm and the cheese is gently melted, about 5 minutes. Garnish with parsley and serve hot or warm.

TO BROIL: Preheat a broiler with the oven rack about 6 inches from the heat. Prepare the peppers as above, but arrange the pepper "gondolas" on a baking sheet. Instead of brushing with olive oil, drizzle the oil over the cheese-topped peppers, then broil. Also, because broiling dries out the anchovies, add them after cooking, before sprinkling on the parsley.

BELLY UP TO THE OLIVE BAR

Like nuts, olives epitomize classic bar food. They're salty finger food, a little exotic, and they come in dozens of varieties—all ready to eat. A quick stop at an olive bar, which even some supermarkets now offer, yields a fun selection of olives to mix and match. Really strong or salt-puckering olives are best for cooking or adding to salads. Personally, I prefer these picks for nibbling at the bar:

• **CERIGNOLA**—Italian; green, huge, firm and meaty; lots of flavor without being salty or bitter

• **GAETA**—Italian; black, small, firm and chewy; medium flavor and saltiness, mildly bitter, but pleasantly so

• **GORDAL OR QUEEN**—Spanish; green, big, firm, tart, and tasty; gordal means "fat," an apt description of these pleasingly plump olives

• **KALAMATA**—Greek; black, large, a bit salty, but also pleasantly tart

• **PICHOLINE**—French; green, small, intensely flavorful, with mild to medium saltiness

Cognac Shrimp Wrapped in Bacon

SERVES 6 AS BAR BITES

Sometimes the most elegant recipes are also the easiest. Here, the sweetness of shrimp blends with the warm flavors of cognac, bacon, and sage. If desired, substitute prosciutto for the bacon. You may also cook these shrimp on an outdoor grill, over medium-high direct heat, for about five minutes per side.

12 jumbo shrimp
¼ cup cognac
12 fresh sage leaves, or 1 teaspoon dried
6 thin slices lean bacon
Freshly ground black pepper
1 lemon, cut in wedges
4 bamboo skewers

1. Remove the shrimp shells but leave the tails on. Devein, if desired. Marinate the shrimp in the cognac for 30 to 60 minutes. If using dried sage, add it to the cognac marinade.

2. Preheat the broiler. Cut the bacon slices in half lengthwise. Drain the shrimp (reserve the marinade; see Note below). Wrap each shrimp in a piece of bacon. Thread the shrimp on skewers, placing fresh sage leaves (if using) in between them. Add a generous grind of pepper. (These may be prepared 1 day in advance, covered, and refrigerated.) Wrap the skewers' ends with foil to prevent burning.

3. Broil for about 5 minutes per side. The shrimp should be just cooked, pink and tender without being tough, and the bacon cooked through. Remove the foil. Serve warm with lemon wedges and garnish with any remaining sage leaves.

NOTE: Boil the reserved cognac marinade and any pan juices from the shrimp for 1 minute. Use this as a sauce (served with bread for sopping it up), or as a base for a pasta side dish, adding olive oil and flavorings of your choice, such as parsley, garlic, and lemon juice.

Port and Paprika Chicken Bites

SERVES 4 AS BAR BITES

Spanish ingredients—port wine, paprika, cilantro, and olive oil—flavor this tapas-style dish. Set out cocktail picks, or toothpicks for nibbling on these delicious little bits. To cook once and enjoy twice, double the recipe (omitting the cilantro) and freeze half. Then just thaw and reheat in a skillet, adding fresh cilantro before serving.

2 cloves garlic

2 bay leaves

3 tablespoons port

2 tablespoons extra-virgin olive oil

1 tablespoon cider vinegar

2 teaspoons sweet paprika

½ teaspoon sea salt

1 pound boneless, skinless chicken thighs, cut in bite-size chunks (about 1 inch square)

½ cup chopped cilantro (chop just before cooking)

½ cup diced onion (small dice)

1. Grind the garlic and bay leaves together in the work bowl of a hand blender or mini-chopper. (Or chop the garlic by hand and finely crumble the bay leaves, then mix with the remaining ingredients.) Add the port, 1 tablespoon of the olive oil, the vinegar, paprika, and salt, then blend together until well mixed. Marinate the chicken in the mixture 1 to 2 hours.

2. Just before cooking, chop enough cilantro to make ½ cup. Spread the cilantro out on a serving plate.

3. To cook the chicken, heat the remaining 1 tablespoon of olive oil on high in a wok or large skillet. With a slotted spoon, scoop the chicken pieces out of the marinade and into the hot oil, arranging them in a single layer. Cook until they brown on the bottom, 2 to 3 minutes, then stir-fry them until cooked through, 2 to 3 minutes more. Scoop the chicken bits out of the pan, leaving excess oil behind, and place them in a single layer on the bed of cilantro.

4. Add the onion to the hot pan, return the pan to the heat, and cook, stirring, until browned on the edges, about 2 minutes. Scoop the onion out of the oil and sprinkle on the chicken. Serve the plate of chicken bites hot or at room temperature, sprinkled with a touch of salt, and with cocktail picks or toothpicks for handling.

TAPAS BARS

Spaniards go to bars to converse, join friends, argue, joke, and flirt. Tapas are provided to keep them going. Spaniards eat dinner late, very late, as late as midnight, but usually ten o'clock is the dining hour (and two o'clock is lunch). Tapas, which means "assorted little dishes," fill the gap, as midday or after-work snacks served with glasses of sherry on the side.

Tapar means "to cover," and the first tapa was a slice of ham served on top of a sherry glass, reportedly to keep out the flies. Barkeeps discovered that the saltiness of the ham spurred beverage sales, and a tradition was born. Every region has its own specialty tapas, and because tapas are typically simple dishes, the success of a great tapa depends almost entirely on the quality of its ingredients.

Envision this:

. . . It's 8:00 p.m. and you're at a tapas bar in Madrid. Patrons are lined up at the bar, calling their orders to the bartender. In minutes, the crowd swells and the patrons spill out onto the street, carrying their glasses and tapas with them. You elbow your way in and imme-

diately are seduced by the aromas of garlic, olive oil, shellfish, ham, cheese, and saffron wafting from handmade pottery bowls. The last bar you were in listed their tapas on the wall, but here, patrons just take what they want, keeping track of their own treats as the evening drives on, and paying before they leave. In some bars, tapas are served on toothpicks, and these are used to tally the bill. You eyeball the bowls and start to take your first round of tapas. It's hard to tell what some of them are, but here's what you end up with: Chickpeas and Spinach; Clams and Chorizo; Meatballs in Almond Sauce; Valdeon Cheese and Pears; Grilled Pork; Octopus Salad; and Quail with Onions.

That's more than enough for now—you still have dinner ahead!

Salmon Cassis

SERVES 2 TO 3 AS A LIGHT ENTREE

This bistro-style dish makes a perfect light lunch or supper, eaten al fresco under shady umbrellas, preceded by a glass of Kir, a refreshing summertime drink that consists of white wine splashed with crème de cassis, a black currant-flavored liqueur. Crème de cassis also plays a pivotal role in these simple salmon strips, yielding a rich, caramelized glaze with sweet and fruity tones, accented by a soy sauce splash. For a complete meal, serve the salmon strips with lightly dressed mesclun greens, and a crusty baguette on the side.

1 pound salmon fillet, preferably with skin
3 tablespoons crème de cassis
2 tablespoons soy sauce
4 teaspoons extra-virgin olive oil
1 clove garlic, minced
Freshly ground black pepper
Minced chives or sesame seeds for garnish
  (optional)

1. Place the salmon skin-side down on a cutting board. Slice the salmon in half, to make two mirror images. Slice each of these pieces in half lengthwise, to create four identical, narrow salmon strips.

2. Combine the cassis, soy sauce, 2 teaspoons of the olive oil, and the garlic in a shallow dish. Add the salmon, turning to coat on all sides. Sprinkle it generously with pepper. Marinate, refrigerated, for about 1 hour, turning halfway through.

3. Heat the remaining 2 teaspoons of olive oil in a skillet or grill pan over medium-high heat until very hot. Place the salmon pieces in the pan, with one of the fleshy sides down. Cook 1 minute, until the cooked surface is brown and caramelized. Flip the pieces over to cook the other fleshy side, and cook another minute until it also is richly colored. Gently turn the pieces skin-side down and cook for about 1 minute more, just to crisp the skin. Gently remove the salmon to a serving plate.

4. Pour any remaining marinade into the pan and cook, stirring up any browned bits, until it forms a syrupy glaze. Serve the salmon warm or at room temperature, drizzled with the pan glaze. If desired, garnish with minced chives or sesame seeds.

Cocoa Nib Wine Points with Pasilla Spice

MAKES 40 POINTS

Cocoa nibs, essentially raw chocolate from the cocoa bean, put a crunchy, pleasantly bitter spin into these addictive little nibbles. Enhanced with a mild dose of fruity pasilla chile, olive oil, and red wine, these savory bites add a slightly sweet, slightly spicy snap to wine and beer. They're especially good with red wine, dark beer, or some of the specialty fruit ales. Use a rich red wine with lots of flavor, like a cabernet, for these crunchy bites.

This recipe lets you slice the dough free-form, into wedge-shaped points, but you can also use a two-inch biscuit cutter. Pasilla chile is raisin-like and mild; for more chile flavor, increase the amount or add a pinch of cayenne. Look for cocoa nibs, also called cacao nibs, at specialty food stores or in bakers' catalogs.

1 cup all-purpose flour, preferably unbleached
¼ cup plus 1 teaspoon sugar
1 teaspoon ground pasilla chile
½ teaspoon salt
1½ teaspoons baking powder
¼ cup red wine
3 tablespoons extra virgin olive oil
1 heaping tablespoon cocoa (cacao) nibs, plus extra for garnish
1 large egg white beaten with 1 teaspoon water

1. Stir the flour, sugar, chile, salt, and baking powder together in a mixing bowl. Mix in the red wine and olive oil. Using your hands, mix in the 1 tablespoon of cocoa nibs and form the dough into a ball. Refrigerate for 10 minutes.

2. While the dough rests, preheat the oven to 350°F. Lightly grease a baking sheet (preferably nonstick, about 17×12 inches or similar size) with olive oil.

3. Roll the dough into disks, 3–4 inches in diameter and about ¼ inch thick. Slice each disk into 6 wedge-shaped points. Scrape up excess dough and reroll until all dough is used. Place the points on the baking sheet at least ½ inch apart. You should get around 40 points, but if you end up with more or less, that's okay, too.

(continued)

4. For each point, brush the top with the egg-white mixture, then garnish with 4 or 5 cocoa nibs and lightly tap them down with your fingertip. Bake 15 to 17 minutes, until the edges are lightly browned. Let cool completely on the tray. Points may be stored airtight for 2 weeks, if they last that long, or freeze up to 3 months.

BREWPUB NIBBLES AND NOSHES

Casual conversation, a glance around the room to see which regulars are in tonight, and the malty aroma of freshly brewed beer . . .

The neighborhood brewpub has returned. Hurrah! It's a little brighter and shinier than its forebears, which fed the Founding Fathers, gold rushers, sailors in port, and the grain-growers of the plains. Some might say the small-batch brews are better, too—nut-brown ales, fruity lambics, porters, pilsners, lagers, and bocks. Complex and refreshing, inventive and enticing. Old-world beers redesigned to be served with the new world of food and cooking. Fortunately, a great many craft beers can be toted home, either directly from the brewery or icy cold from the market.

Certain foods almost demand to be washed down by a chilled ale or a cool stout. Mexican *antojitos*, Southern barbecue, spicy sausages, hearty breads, aged cheeses, and deep-fried-anything qualify—and can taste even better when the brew is cooked into the food.

Kyoto Chips

SERVES 3 TO 4

This East-West combination is a bit like lounging in worn blue jeans and a Japanese hapi coat: It's homey, comfy, and a little offbeat, but it works. And it's so easy. Simply heat potato chips in an oven, then toss them with a savory Japanese seasoning known as furikake.

Furikake is traditionally sprinkled on rice, but I use it on everything from soup to nuts, and as a seasoning in panko-coated foods. The basic ingredients are dried seaweed (nori), sesame seeds, salt, and sugar, with such flavoring variations as wasabi, dried bonito, salmon, or shiso. Pick up a jar at Asian markets or gourmet grocers.

In this recipe, instead of shaking the furikake directly from the jar, as is typically the case, grind it to a powder in a spice grinder, food processor, or blender, so it better adheres to the chips. If you have a toaster oven, cook the recipe in two batches, or just make half of it.

Besides pairing well with beer—or really any drink—these chips also match the exotic appeal of chilled jun mai sake. (Sake, being brewed, is technically a beer anyway, though most folks treat it as wine.)

One 9-ounce bag plain potato chips (kettle-style or other good quality)
3 to 4 tablespoons furikake

1. Preheat the oven to 350°F. While the oven heats, finely grind the furikake (in a spice grinder, food processor, or blender).

2. Spread the chips on a baking sheet and cook for 4 to 5 minutes. When you see oil on the chips, remove them from the oven and sprinkle them with the ground furikake to taste. Serve hot or at room temperature. Store in an airtight container for up to 1 week.

THE EAGLE HAS CROSSED THE POND: GASTROPUBS INVADE U.S.

In 1991, London hatched the world's first "gastropub," and fortunately it spawned a league of imitators, first in England and now in the United States. Two gents, David Eyre and Mike Belben, converted a run-down pub called the Eagle into a novel concept: They kept the coziness of a traditional pub but added the gastronomy of fresh, local food with a robust kick. To this day, the Eagle's food is as simple and honest as the surroundings—an atmosphere of comfortable sofas, mismatched tables and chairs, and blackboard menus, with an open kitchen—but it's hardly old-fashioned pub fare.

Traditional pubs have always been neighborly meeting places, fueled by ale and food at reasonable prices. But a gastropub serves its fare with an Alice Waters–Chez Panisse sensibility, offering delicious, seasonal dishes from innovative chefs. British food has never tasted so good. Actress Kate Winslet even held her wedding reception at a gastropub. In the United States, gastropubs with their own unique menus are popping up in big cities everywhere, offering plenty of inspiration for devising more great bar food at home. New York's The Spotted Pig became an early hot spot for high-profile clientele (including one of its own investors, Mario Batali), and Hollywood chef Ben Ford (son of actor Harrison Ford) was among the first to open gastropubs stateside, first in Tulsa and then in Culver City, a movie enclave of Los Angeles.

Creamy Gouda-Horseradish Spread

MAKES ABOUT 3 CUPS

This zesty spread comes together in minutes with the use of a food processor, and if you have it, an electric mixer. Serve it on crackers or small breads, as a canapé base, or as a knockout sandwich spread, especially with roast beef.

The better the Gouda, the sharper the taste. Aged Goudas have a wonderfully rich, nutty flavor. For convenience, though, the small, seven-ounce waxed wheels of May-Bud Gouda, in supermarket deli cases, are the perfect size for this recipe, taste fine, and last a long time in the fridge, ready to be whipped into this spread at any time.

¾ cup heavy cream
2 cloves garlic
2 ounces regular or reduced-fat cream cheese, softened
7 ounces Gouda cheese (about 2 cups shredded)
3 tablespoons prepared horseradish
1½ teaspoons white wine vinegar
½ teaspoon ground white pepper
¼ teaspoon salt
Coarsely ground black pepper

1. With an electric mixer or by hand, whip the cream just until it forms stiff peaks. (For a small amount of cream like this, use a narrow bowl, rather than a wide one.)

2. Using a food processor, drop peeled garlic cloves into the feed tube while the machine runs. Process until the garlic is chopped. Cut the cream cheese into chunks and add them to the garlic in the work bowl. Add the Gouda, horseradish, vinegar, white pepper, and salt. Process until the mixture is completely smooth, scraping down the sides of the work bowl as needed. Using the pulse button, process in the whipped cream just until blended. Cover and chill at least 2 hours, preferably overnight, for the flavors to blend. The spread will keep for 1 week refrigerated. Before serving, garnish with black pepper and bring to room temperature for fullest flavor.

Cumin-Cheddar Coins

MAKES 40 TO 50 WAFERS

These are delicate little nibbles that pack plenty of punch. They're great with cocktails or just by themselves, and they're especially tasty with beer (Cheddar, cumin, and beer are like a holy trinity of flavors). Adjust the amount of red pepper flakes to your preferred heat level; half a teaspoon will be subtle, and one teaspoon is delightfully detectable.

4 ounces shredded sharp Cheddar cheese (about 1 cup packed)
¼ cup soft goat cheese (chèvre), about 2.5 ounces
¼ cup (½ stick) salted butter, in 4 chunks
½ cup all-purpose flour
2 tablespoons cornmeal
1 teaspoon cumin seeds
½ to 1 teaspoon crushed red pepper flakes
¼ teaspoon salt

1. Preheat the oven to 350°F. Lightly grease a baking sheet. For easier mixing, let all ingredients come to room temperature.

2. In a large bowl, stir together all ingredients until loosely combined. Continue mixing by hand, until the mixture forms a pliable, uniform dough (soft, like Play-Doh). Roll into two logs, each about 1 inch in diameter and 6 inches long. Bake now, or for firmer dough, wrap each log in plastic wrap and refrigerate at least 1 hour, or 1 day in advance. (Logs may also be frozen up to 1 month; thaw in refrigerator before slicing and baking.)

3. When ready to bake, slice each log into ¼- to ⅓-inch wafers and place on the greased baking sheet. Bake 15 to 18 minutes, until the edges start to look toasty. Loosen the wafers with a spatula and transfer to a plate to cool. Store airtight for up to 1 week. (Baked wafers may be frozen up to 2 months. Thaw at room temperature before serving.)

THERE'S NO FREE LUNCH—
BUT THERE USED TO BE

Prior to Prohibition, saloons and bars competed for customers by offering free lunch buffets. Few lunches were actually free, but for a mere nickel tossed into a cigar box, or 30 cents for a five-course businessman's lunch, the price was nominal—as long as you were drinking. The foods served were intentionally salty and spicy, encouraging another drink, and if you aimed to eat without drinking, the trusty bouncer would give you "the bum's rush."

According to historian James Trager, Delmonico's in New York served hard-cooked eggs with caviar, lobster, roast beef, pickled walnuts, and Kentucky ham. Neighborhood saloons set up more modest spreads on long wooden bars, with pickled pigs' feet, sardines, hard cheese, and cold cuts. McSorley's Old Ale House, the longest-running saloon in New York (since 1854), still serves raw onions, sharp cheese, hot mustard, deli meats, and dark rye bread—but for a bit more than a nickel.

When Prohibition arrived and patrons went underground to do their drinking, pubs, saloons, and many of New York's finest eateries closed their doors forever, unable to survive on food alone. The free lunch died with them.

In the thirteen years that beer was outlawed, the consumer's taste changed. Any beer, no matter how watered down or flavorless, was welcome. New laws kept a beer's alcohol content low, and after the Great Depression, the nickel that once bought a full meal at a saloon now barely mustered up a short glass of beer.

Today's small breweries revived the demand for flavorful beers. They may not offer a free lunch, but the most successful ones discovered that the better the food they serve, the more beer they sell—a practice that would have happened earlier, had it not been for some pesky laws prohibiting breweries from operating taverns on the same premises. When most states did away with those laws in the 1980s, the modern brewpub was born.

HOW MEXICO GOT ITS BEER

When Mexicans initiated the first Cinco de Mayo party, celebrating their 1862 victory over the French at the Battle of Puebla, they toasted not with beer or tequila, but tossed down viscous shots of milky white *pulque*—fermented cactus juice that is undisputedly an acquired taste.

I first sipped pulque in a ramshackle, mud-plastered hut somewhere in central Mexico. Made from the maguey or century plant, pulque is a desperate, rustic drink. Local pulquerias served it to farmers and the working class as a low-octane buzz for just a few pesos. The Aztecs reserved it solely for religious ceremonies. When the Spaniards came along, pulque evolved into popular street tipple, with pulquerias popping up in almost every neighborhood. Today, pulque has been largely replaced by its close relatives, mescal and tequila, and European-style beer. But where did the beer come from?

In a complicated historical hiccup, Austrian immigrants brought their brewery skills to Mexico right around the time of the original Cinco de Mayo battle. Napoleon had dispatched

his cousin, Archduke Maximilian of Austria, to conquer Mexico in the name of the French. The Mexicans rebelled, and a surprisingly small band defeated Maximilian"s army at Puebla on May 5, 1862. Austria's Max was soon slain, but Austrians and Germans continued to arrive, bringing accordions, waltzes, and polkas (which evolved into hybrid conjunto bands and *música norteña*)—and turned their beer-making skills into a national industry. Though some connoisseurs view Mexico's light lagers as the lowly brew of beach bunnies, frat jocks, and commercial hype, others hold the dark lagers of Austrian pedigree in high regard, particularly Negra Modelo and the Christmas brew Noche Buena.

Spanish Smoked Paprika Wings

SERVES 4 AS BAR BITES

In this super-easy recipe, wing pieces roast in just a few well-chosen spices until they're golden-crisp and completely irresistible. Supermarkets sell packages of chicken wing pieces, either the center pieces or drummettes, with the tips already removed.

If you've never cooked with it before, lusty Spanish smoked paprika will change your life. Find it in specialty food stores, or order it online. I prefer the sweet, mild (rather than hot) variety for this finger-food dish, but take your pick. Even regular unsmoked paprika makes a bold statement, so don't skip over this recipe just because smoked paprika isn't handy.

2 teaspoons ground cumin
1 teaspoon granulated (or powdered) garlic
1 teaspoon dried marjoram, crushed
1 teaspoon paprika, preferably Spanish smoked paprika
1 teaspoon salt
2 pounds chicken wing pieces
2 tablespoons olive oil

1. Preheat the oven to 425°F.

2. Mix together the cumin, garlic, marjoram, paprika, and salt in a small bowl. Rinse the chicken pieces and pat dry. Rub the spice mixture all over the chicken. Pour the olive oil onto a large baking sheet and spread it around. Roll the chicken pieces in the oil until lightly coated on all sides, then arrange them neatly in a single layer without touching.

3. Bake for 20 minutes. Flip the pieces over and bake for another 20 to 25 minutes. They should be slightly crisp and golden on the outside. Serve hot or at room temperature.

Santa Fe–Caesar Crema

MAKES ABOUT 1 1/2 CUPS

This lively avocado mixture can be a dip or a spread, depending on how you use it. Set a small bowl of it out with bagel chips, garlic toasts, or small romaine leaves, or spoon it over taquitos or mini-tacos. It's got the spirit of old Santa Fe with the flavor punch of a Caesar salad.

2 cloves garlic
1/2 cup packed fresh cilantro
3 canned anchovy fillets, or to taste
1 large ripe avocado
2 tablespoons fresh lime juice
2 tablespoons fresh lemon juice
1/2 cup regular or low-fat sour cream
1/4 cup finely grated Parmesan cheese
1 teaspoon extra-virgin olive oil
1/4 teaspoon Worcestershire sauce
Coarsely ground black pepper

1. With the food processor running, peel and drop the garlic cloves, cilantro, and anchovies into the feed tube and process until the garlic is finely chopped. Cut open the avocado and scoop the flesh into the food processor bowl. Pour the lime and lemon juices and sour cream over the avocado. Pulse just long enough to mix up the avocado (chunks are okay; contact with the acids helps prevent the avocado from turning brown).

2. Add the Parmesan, olive oil, and Worcestershire. Pulse until well blended with little green cilantro flecks. Taste to correct the seasonings. Garnish with pepper. Serve now or refrigerate to serve later or the next day. Bring to room temperature for fullest flavor. (The crema will last 3 days, but the flavors will diminish over time.)

Nachos Grandes with Chorizo and Artichokes

SERVES 6 AS BAR BITES

Authentic nachos contain quality fixings: real aged cheese, freshly fried tortilla chips, and fresh jalapeños (no neon-orange sloppy-sauce). In my book *Macho Nachos*, I developed dozens of ways to dress up the nacho and still retain its integrity as good food, not junk food. In my latest rendition, Spanish chorizo from the Old World meets New World nacho ingredients.

Be sure to use Spanish chorizo, a cured paprika-spiced hard sausage easily found in gourmet markets—not Mexican chorizo, which is tasty but raw and needs cooking. Peel away the paper-thin casing before slicing.

For a splashy presentation, serve a single "nacho grande" per person. Also known as tostadas, they're simply whole tortillas, freshly fried (or buy them pre-fried from Mexican markets or from a Mexican restaurant), instead of smaller tortilla chips. The whole tortillas are less time consuming (no need to top each chip). Plus, a really big nacho just looks so inviting! (But if you prefer to use tortilla chips, that's okay.)

¾ cup coarsely chopped marinated artichoke hearts
¼ cup finely chopped Italian parsley
Vegetable or other oil for deep-frying
Four 6-inch corn tortillas
3 tablespoons sun-dried tomato pesto
6 ounces shredded Monterey Jack cheese
¼ cup thinly sliced, skinned Spanish chorizo
(casera-style)

1. Preheat the oven to 475°F, with an oven rack in the top third of the oven.

2. Combine the artichoke hearts and parsley in a small bowl and set aside.

3. In a deep-fat fryer or heavy pot, heat the oil to 375°F. (Pour enough oil into the pot to measure a depth of 1 inch, or follow the fryer manufacturer's instructions.) Deep-fry the corn tortillas, turning once, until crisp and golden, 2 to 3 minutes. Drain on paper towels. (These can be stored airtight for up to 3 days.) Line a baking sheet with nonstick foil (or regular foil spritzed with nonstick spray). Arrange the fried tortillas on the foil.

4. Top the tortillas with the pesto (smear or dot it on as best you can), followed by the cheese, then by the chorizo. Bake for 6 to 8 minutes, until the cheese browns lightly and bubbles. Spoon the artichoke mixture on top and serve hot with plenty of napkins.

====================

GIVE ME SOME GARLIC AND CRACKER JACK . . .

Hot dogs and beer were once the leading icons of baseball stadium food. But over the past century, various competitors to the dog came along. In 1975, Texas Stadium started hawking gloppy orange cheese sauce on chips, forever distorting our concept of true nachos. Recently, a far more satisfying snack has dogged the dog: garlic fries. Some say these crispy, steaming hot French fries, sprinkled with garlic, parsley, and kosher salt, originated in brewpubs, and indeed, the Gordon Biersch brewery chain is famous for its version. Stadium vendors soon caught on that beer and garlic fries were a combined hit, striking other foods right out of the park. Today, some San Diego Padres and Seattle Mariners fans claim to have converted to baseball solely because of the garlic fries. Purportedly the best garlic fries are found in San Francisco's baseball stadium, where they're liberally doused with fresh garlic from the nearby fields of Gilroy, self-proclaimed garlic capital of the world.

Make your own Authentic Garlic Fries on page 106, or the baked version, Cheaters' Garlic Fries, on page 108.

Authentic Garlic Fries

SERVES 4

This is the real deal. They're a bit more involved than the Cheaters' Garlic Fries on page 108, but if you've got the time and the craving, they're worth the effort. Both recipes use the same flavorings, but the cheaters' version leisurely bakes the fries as wedges, so they're more soft and tender, instead of deep-frying them into these traditional crispy, crunchy sticks.

2 pounds russet (baking) potatoes, scrubbed
2 tablespoons finely chopped garlic
¼ cup olive oil
Vegetable or other oil for deep-frying
⅓ cup chopped fresh parsley
Sea salt and freshly ground black pepper

1. Slice the potatoes (skin on) into ⅜-inch-thick fries. Rinse, drain, and pat dry.

2. Mix the garlic with the olive oil and set aside.

3. In a deep-fat fryer or heavy pot, heat the vegetable oil to 375°F. Deep-fry the potatoes (in batches if necessary) for 5 minutes. Drain on paper towels. At this point, they can rest for up to 2 hours at room temperature.

4. Reheat the oil to the same temperature (375°F), and refry the potatoes for 2 to 3 minutes, until crisp and golden. Toss the potatoes in a large bowl with the garlic-oil mixture, chopped parsley, and a generous amount of salt and pepper.

Cheaters' Garlic Fries

SERVES 6 TO 8 AS BAR BITES

True garlic fries, the kind served at San Francisco ball parks and Gordon Biersch Brewery, can be hard to pass up. However, serving them at home may be more demanding than the average person cares to attempt. It's not that they're difficult to make at home, but as bar food, they're a bit tedious (slicing, rinsing, and drying the fries, then frying them not just once, but twice, before tossing them with garlic, olive oil, and parsley). You could bake up frozen garlic fries, but what they gain in convenience they lose in flavor. I've come up with a fresh, robust alternative that never fails to be devoured, and takes just a few minutes of actual labor. These guys are crisp, garlicky, and good on the outside and soft and delicate inside. Set out a tray as bar snacks, or serve as a side dish with steaks and chops.

2 pounds russet potatoes, scrubbed and
    dried but not peeled
6 tablespoons extra virgin olive oil
1 teaspoon freshly ground black pepper, or
    more to taste
1½ teaspoons sea salt, or more to taste
2 tablespoons minced garlic
2 tablespoons minced parsley

1. Preheat the oven to 425°F. Slice each potato in half lengthwise. Then cut each half lengthwise into 6 to 8 wedges (the thinner the wedges, the crisper the outer surface).

2. Set out a baking sheet with low sides. Pour 3 tablespoons of the olive oil into the baking sheet. Pile the potato wedges onto the pan, and with your hands, move the potatoes around in the oil until all sides are coated. Arrange the wedges in columns, standing them on their curved sides. Sprinkle with pepper. (The potatoes may prepared to this stage up to 1 hour before cooking.) Sprinkle with salt just before baking.

3. Bake about 45 minutes. While the potatoes cook, combine the remaining 3 tablespoons of olive oil and the garlic. About 3 minutes before the potatoes are done, when they have already browned on the edges and sides, stir the parsley into the garlic-oil mixture. Drizzle over the potatoes and bake for another 3 to 5 minutes. Pull the tray from the oven before the garlic browns, or it will taste bitter. Taste, and sprinkle with more salt if needed. Serve immediately.

Caraway Kefta

MAKES 8 KEFTA

From Armenia to Arabia, seasoned ground meat "fingers," known as kefta, are enjoyed as either main meals or little dishes. They're typically molded around flat skewers and grilled, but this version pan-fries the kefta in olive oil until crisp and brown.

Caraway seed, frequently found in European rye breads, actually originated in Asia some five thousand years ago, and its Western name derives from karawya, as it's known in Arabic. Reminiscent of lemon, anise, and pepper, caraway seed is the only seasoning needed here to accent the onion, flatbread, and sesame flavors, along with a bit of salt and pepper.

Tip: The kefta will, like hamburger patties, shrink on the outside and puff in the center as they cook. For a flatter kefta, roll the meat into balls, flatten them slightly, then press your thumb down to leave a depression in the center.

½ pound extra-lean ground lamb or beef
2 tablespoons finely chopped onion, preferably red onion
2 tablespoons sesame seeds
½ teaspoon caraway seeds
¼ to ½ teaspoon salt
¼ teaspoon fresh coarsely ground black pepper
1 to 2 teaspoons olive oil
2 pita breads, quartered; or 8 mini-pita breads, warmed in a low oven
Yogurt, for serving
Sliced sweet or red onion, cucumbers, tomatoes, and lettuce, for serving

1. Using your hands, mix together the meat, onion, sesame seeds, caraway seeds, ¼ teaspoon of the salt, and the pepper. When the mixture feels like it will hold together, shape it into 8 patties, or flattened meatballs. (The kefta mixture may be combined and shaped 1 day in advance and refrigerated. You can also precook the kefta the day before, leaving them slightly undercooked, then reheat in a skillet with a little oil.)

2. Thinly film a medium-size skillet with olive oil, just enough to coat. Heat over medium-high heat. Add the kefta and brown on all sides until the interior is cooked through, but still slightly pink in the center, 4 to 5 minutes. (Taste a small nibble, and sprinkle on more salt if needed.)

3. To serve, stuff each bread pocket with kefta and yogurt, and add onion, cucumbers, tomatoes, and lettuce, as desired.

Char Shu Slices with Mahogany Marmalade and Hot Mustard

SERVES 6 AS BAR BITES

This bar-food version of sliced pork echoes the glazed pieces that hang in Chinatown restaurant windows. Sliced char shu is meant to be enjoyed at room temperature, and can be made a day or two before slicing and serving.

The instructions are detailed but the process is not complicated in the least. You marinate the pork, broil it until almost done, baste with the reduced marinade, finish under the broiler, and slice when cool. Then serve with hot mustard and the reduced "marmalade."

1 pork tenderloin (1 to 1¼ pounds)
¼ cup soy sauce
3 tablespoons molasses
2 tablespoons hoisin sauce
2 tablespoons triple sec or dry sherry (optional)
2 cloves garlic, minced
2 finely chopped scallions (green and white parts)
1-inch piece fresh ginger, minced
1 tablespoon toasted sesame oil
Hot Mustard, for serving (see Note)

1. Cut the tenderloin into 2 equal, short, plump pieces for easier handling and quicker cooking. In a shallow baking dish or a resealable plastic bag, combine the soy sauce, molasses, hoisin, triple sec or sherry (if using), garlic, scallion, ginger, and sesame oil. Mix well to dissolve the hoisin and molasses. Add the pork and coat completely. Marinate, refrigerated, for 2 hours to overnight, turning the pork occasionally in the marinade.

2. Preheat the broiler. While the broiler heats, line a baking sheet with nonstick foil, or spritz regular foil with nonstick spray.

3. Place the pork on the foil-lined baking sheet. Pour the marinade into a saucepan, bring it to a boil over medium-high heat, and boil, stirring often, until it reduces to a very thick, syrupy glaze, about 5 minutes. When it cools slightly, the sauce will resemble a marmalade, dense and sweet with bits of scallion, garlic, and ginger.

(continued)

4. Broil the pork for 5 to 7 minutes, until the top side takes on color and starts to look cooked. Turn the pieces over and broil another 5 minutes. Spoon some of the thickened sauce over the pork, coating the top and all sides. Broil for another 3 to 6 minutes, until the glaze caramelizes and turns a deep mahogany color, and the pork is just cooked through. (Pork is done when the internal temperature reaches 160°F. At this temperature, the interior will still be pale pink but safe to eat.)

5. Let the pork rest at least 10 minutes before slicing. You can let it can stand at room temperature for 1 hour, or cover and refrigerate up to 2 days before slicing. To serve, slice the pork at an angle and overlap the slices on a plate. Accompany with a small dish of the reduced "marmalade," a small dish of hot mustard, and soy sauce. Supply each diner with a plate for the pork and marmalade, and a small dish (like a wasabi dish used for sushi) for mixing the mustard with the soy sauce. Use chopsticks (or small forks) to dip the pork into the sauces.

HOT MUSTARD: Mix together 2 teaspoons each dry mustard (or Chinese powdered mustard) and water until smooth. Let the mixture rest 10 to 30 minutes before serving.

Beer-Bathed Shrimp

SERVES 4 TO 6 AS BAR BITES

Pick your own ways to season this recipe, if you like, but don't skip simmering the shrimp shells in the cooking liquid. They're the backbone of both the cooking and the marinating flavors (and besides, you were just going to throw the shells out anyway). The recipe may seem detailed, but it's really simple. Plus, you can make it a full three days in advance.

You may serve these shrimp plain, as finger food, with a squirt of lime, but they also lend themselves to more colorful presentations, such as arranging them on a bed of avocado, tomato, and watercress. Or, hang the shrimp around the edges of shallow bowls or glasses filled with some of the marinating mixture, and serve with slices of French bread to sop up the juices.

One 12-ounce bottle beer (lager or amber ale)
¼ cup cider vinegar
3 cloves garlic, crushed
1 tablespoon pickling spice
½ teaspoon salt
1 pound large shrimp (25 to 30), with shells
½ cup chopped red onion
¼ cup fresh lime juice
2 tablespoons extra-virgin olive oil
1 lime, cut in wedges (optional)
2 tablespoons chopped fresh parsley or cilantro (optional)

1. Combine the beer, vinegar, garlic, spice, and salt in a medium saucepan. Pull the shells off the shrimp but leave the tails on, and toss the shells into the pan as you go. Devein the shrimp while you heat up the liquid mixture: Bring the mixture to a boil over medium heat. Reduce the heat, cover, and simmer over low heat, shaking the pan around occasionally to mix, for 25 minutes. With a slotted spoon, scoop out the shells and large bits of pickling spices, leaving the liquid in the pan.

2. Turn the heat to high and bring the liquid to a rolling boil. Add the shrimp and stir them around with the spoon as they cook (the liquid level will be too low to cover them, so stirring helps cook them evenly). When the shrimp are pink and start to curl (1 to 2 minutes; don't wait for the liquid to return to a boil), scoop them out of the liquid and into a colander in the sink, reserving the cooking liquid. Rinse the shrimp in cold water until cool.

(continued)

3. While the shrimp cool and drain, prepare the marinade. Strain ½ cup of the cooking liquid into a marinating container (I use a jar or plastic container with a tight-sealing lid, so I can shake the shrimp around). Stir in the onion, lime juice, and olive oil. Stir in the shrimp and mix well. Cover and refrigerate, stirring occasionally, for at least 6 hours or up to 36 hours.

4. Serve garnished with lime wedges and chopped herbs, if desired.

Saffron Queso Flameado

SERVES 4 AS BAR BITES

Few bites appeal as much as melted cheese spooned into small tortillas. Use any good melting cheeses, but make sure they're not overly salty. Monterey Jack, mozzarella, and Muenster are good picks. Traditionally, this dish mixes cooked Mexican chorizo and poblano pepper strips in with the cheese, but this simpler version omits them and shines with the flavor and color of saffron instead. For a fancier presentation, set out a small plate of finely diced vegetables to sprinkle into the tortilla with the cheese.

1 tablespoon extra-virgin olive oil
⅛ teaspoon saffron threads
2 tablespoons chopped onion
8 ounces Muenster cheese, diced in 1-inch cubes
8 ounces mozzarella cheese, diced in 1-inch cubes
4 flour and/or corn tortillas, warmed
Finely diced red bell pepper, scallions, and tomatoes for garnish (optional)

1. Preheat the oven to 400°F. Measure the olive oil into a shallow microwave-safe pan (a ceramic tart or glass pie pan works great). Crumble in the saffron and stir in the onion. Microwave on High until the onion softens and the saffron colors the oil, about 1 minute. (Or, cook the mixture on the stove in an ovenproof skillet.)

2. Stir the cheese cubes around in the saffron oil. Bake in the oven 10 to 15 minutes, until the cheese is completely melted, bubbly, and brown on the edges and top. Spoon into soft tortillas and eat plain, or with the suggested garnishes, if desired.

117

Thai Larb with Melon

SERVES 4 AS BAR BITES

Summer in Thailand can be excruciatingly hot—perfect weather to enjoy a cold beer and the cooling mint leaves, cilantro, lemongrass, and lime of this dish. Lamb is especially flavorful, but ground beef and ground turkey work fine, too. Try serving it with a large block of watermelon. The sweet, juicy melon is a harmonious complement to the saltiness, citrus, and spiciness of the larb.

Look for Asian fish sauce (nam pla or nuac mam) and lemongrass in Southeast Asian markets, and sometimes in regular supermarkets. Discard the tough outer layers of the lemongrass and mince only the lower two inches of the stalk, the part that's lavender and white in color. Or substitute lemon zest for the lemongrass. Depending on your preference, the ingredients in this recipe may be finely chopped by hand or by machine (food processor, mini-chopper, or a hand blender's chopping attachment).

3 tablespoons plus 1 teaspoon Asian fish sauce
2 tablespoons water
2 tablespoons plus 2 teaspoons fresh lime juice
2 teaspoons sugar
4 cloves garlic, minced
½ teaspoon crushed red pepper flakes
4 scallions (green and white parts), minced
1 tablespoon minced lemongrass (or lemon zest)
1 pound extra-lean ground lamb or beef
⅓ cup fresh mint leaves, minced
⅓ cup cilantro leaves, minced
Watermelon or cantaloupe chunks, cucumber slices, or crisp lettuce leaves, for garnish

1. Make the dressing: Mix together 1 tablespoon plus 1 teaspoon of the fish sauce, the water, 2 teaspoons of the lime juice, 1 teaspoon of the sugar, ⅛ teaspoon of the minced garlic, and a dash of crushed red pepper flakes (or to taste) in a small bowl until the sugar dissolves, and set aside. (If making the meat in advance, prepare the dressing right before serving, to keep the flavors fresh and crisp.)

2. Stir the remaining 2 tablespoons fish sauce, 2 tablespoons of the lime juice, 1 teaspoon of the sugar, the scallions, the remaining minced garlic, the lemongrass, and the remaining red pepper flakes together in a mixing bowl.

3. Fry the meat in a skillet over medium-high heat, breaking it up, until crumbly. Remove with a slotted spoon and place it in the mixing bowl with the lime juice mixture, leaving excess fat behind (discard the fat).

4. Mash the mixture with a fork to break it into even smaller pieces. Mix in the mint and cilantro. If not serving immediately, refrigerate. (This dish can be prepared 1 day in advance and refrigerated. Bring to room temperature before serving.)

5. Stir in a bit of the reserved dressing, to taste, to enhance the flavors. Serve on small plates, with melon, cucumber, or lettuce and the remaining dressing on the side.

OKTOBERFEST: OOMPA!

Many communities outside Germany celebrate Oktoberfest in October, but in Munich, the festivities begin in September and run for sixteen days, ending on the first Sunday in October. Oktoberfest is known by the locals as "Wies'n," a reference to its historic origins.

The tradition dates back to 1810, when Crown Prince Ludwig, later to become King Ludwig I, married Princess Therese of Saxony-Hildburghausen. The citizens of Munich celebrated the event with festivities in the fields in front of the city gates. They partied hearty for sixteen days. The fields were named Theresienwiese ("Theresa's fields") in honor of the Crown Princess, which the locals shortened to "Wies'n."

Tavern Beer Brats 'n' Onions

SERVES 5 AS BAR BITES

Bratwurst and beer go together, and in Wisconsin (the self-proclaimed Bratwurst Capital of the World), the two constitute a seasonal ritual of cooking, eating, and drinking, usually revolving around outdoor grills, pigskins, and ice chests. This recipe, though, brings the brat indoors, tavern-style, braising it in beer, onion, and caraway seed. Serve the brats whole, or slice them up as smaller nibbles, and serve with earthy, whole-grain rolls. Because the beer thickens into a dense sauce, I use a good-quality pilsner, or any beer that's not too strong or too bitter, as the reduction concentrates and intensifies the beer's inherent flavors.

2 tablespoons canola or vegetable oil
5 links bratwurst (about 1¼ pounds)
1 large onion, sliced into rings about ⅓ inch thick
1 teaspoon caraway seeds
One 12-ounce bottle beer
Coarse ground mustard and rolls, for serving

1. Heat 1 tablespoon of the oil in a large skillet over medium-high heat. Brown the bratwurst on all sides (about 5 minutes), but don't cook all the way through. Remove from the pan.

2. Add the remaining tablespoon of oil to the pan, still on medium-high heat. Stir in the onion and caraway seed. Let the onions cook a bit, stirring occasionally. When they've gotten some color and are brown on the edges, pour in 1 cup of the beer. Boil until the liquid barely coats the pan, about 8 minutes.

3. Return the sausages to the pan. Pour in the remaining ½ cup of beer. Cover, reduce the heat, and braise until the sausages are no longer raw in the center, about 5 minutes, flipping them halfway through. Remove the sausages to a serving platter, and raise the heat. Boil, uncovered, until the onions and liquid form a sauce, about 3 minutes. Pour the onion sauce over the sausages. Serve with coarse ground mustard and hot rolls. (If desired, slice the sausages and mix into the onion sauce, then fill the rolls with the mixture and a dab of mustard.)

Smoky Chipotle Chili

MAKES 7 CUPS

Chili champs may disagree, but classic chili con carne doesn't need three dozen ingredients to taste great, and this simple and relatively quick version proves it. This meaty Texas-style chili contains no tomatoes or beans, just seasoned beef and three kinds of chiles, ramped up with cumin, onion, and garlic. The chipotle chiles in adobo sauce (sold in cans in the Mexican food aisle) are actually roasted jalapeños that impart a fiery, spicy, smoky flavor. Sweet paprika adds red chile flavor without heat, and the pasilla chile releases mild fruity, raisin tones.

If you like your chili on fire, add more chipotles with sauce. As chili con carne goes, this is a flavorful but (on the tongue of a chilihead) somewhat tame version. I make it this way intentionally, so I can add the vinegary kick of Tabasco or other hot sauce at table.

1 tablespoon vegetable oil (or bacon grease if you have it)
3 pounds ground beef, preferably half sirloin and half chuck
2 cups chicken broth
4 canned chipotle chiles in adobo, plus 1 to 2 tablespoons adobo sauce
6 cloves garlic, crushed with the flat of a knife
1 large onion, diced
3 tablespoons ground cumin
2 tablespoons sweet (mild) paprika
1 tablespoon ground pasilla chile
1 tablespoon dried oregano, crushed, preferably Mexican
1 tablespoon soy sauce, preferably Kikkoman
1 teaspoon salt, or more to taste
Diced tomatoes, bell peppers, red onion, and if desired, a spoonful of cooked pinto beans or a handful of shredded cheese, for serving

1. In a heavy pot, warm the oil over medium-high heat, then brown the meat over high heat, stirring and breaking up chunks until crumbly.

2. While the meat cooks, pour about $\frac{1}{2}$ cup of chicken broth into the work bowl of a hand blender, mini-chopper, food processor, or blender. Drop in the chipotle chiles and adobo sauce. Puree until smooth. Add the garlic and pulse until it is finely chopped.

(continued)

3. When the meat is crumbly, reduce the heat to medium. Stir in the onion, the chipotle mixture, the remaining 1½ cups chicken broth, the cumin, paprika, pasilla chile, oregano, soy sauce, and salt. Cover and simmer over low heat for about an hour. For best results, let the chili cool, then refrigerate overnight so the flavors blend. Reheat and serve with the accompaniments of your choice. (Refrigerate for up to 3 days, or freeze up to 3 months.)

INDEX